All Kinds of CODES

All Kinds of

by Walt Babson

FOUR WINDS PRESS · NEW YORK

LIBRARY OF CONGRESS CATALOGING IN PUBLICATION DATA

Babson, Walt.
  All kinds of codes.

  Includes index.
  SUMMARY: An introduction to the world of codes and how
to write and break them.
  1. Cryptography—Juvenile literature. 2. Ciphers—Juvenile
literature. [1. Cryptography. 2. Ciphers]
I. Title.
Z103.3.B3   001.54′36   76–17529
ISBN 0–590–07427–X

PUBLISHED BY FOUR WINDS PRESS
A DIVISION OF SCHOLASTIC MAGAZINES, INC., NEW YORK, N.Y.
COPYRIGHT © 1976 BY WALTER BABSON
ALL RIGHTS RESERVED
PRINTED IN THE UNITED STATES OF AMERICA
LIBRARY OF CONGRESS CATALOG CARD NUMBER: 76–17529
1   2   3   4   5   80   79   78   77   76

AV TF MVBY ILZA WHSZ

Ruth, Jim, Amy, Bub and Nan

CONTENTS

Introduction

YEARS AGO, when I was about your age, I went to some of the most lively secret meetings you can imagine. They lasted only fifteen seconds. Instead of sitting down, as you might expect, we all stood up. And, strange as it seems, one of my friends did all the talking—in code.

In case you haven't guessed, these meetings were our huddles, back when I played sandlot football. The code our quarterback reeled off was "X-12-Offtackle" or something like that.

Through the years I've come across hundreds of codes. Many of them, I thought, were ho-hum, as easy to break as a dry stick. Those I've tossed away. The fifty or so that I've finally gathered range from fairly simple mind teasers to those that are as hard to untangle as a string of tight knots. Some are crusty old-timers, going back twenty-five hundred years; others are as new as this book.

I've been wary of big words since the time my mother took me off to our family doctor, after I'd been "beaned" with a baseball. When he told me I had a "temporal contusion" I thought I was as good as dead. Luckily, my mother decoded his message. What I had, she said, was no more than a bump on my head.

Like doctors, code makers and code breakers have their own stock of ten-dollar words—*steganography, cryptography, cryptanalysis, monalphabetic, polyalphabetic*—and such. They *do* serve a useful purpose. If you like big words, you'll come to like these. If not, I've supplied enough ten-centers to take their place.

Since this book is called *All Kinds of Codes,* it has to do with secret writing, homemade secret languages, and code hints about how to improve your memory. Some expert codesters will say that many of these so-called codes are really ciphers. Just to beat them to the punch, I'll agree. Technically, they're right. But this book is, I hope, as nontechnical as it can be.

Most "true" codes are based on nothing more than a big book of words that don't mean what they normally mean. APPLEBLOSSOM, for instance, might be the codeword for *We attack on Friday.* HORSEFLY might mean *At 8 p.m.* To send and receive messages of this kind would require a codebook for you and each of your friends, and would be as dreary a way to pass the time as I can imagine.

Most of the codes (or ciphers) in this book are a far

more lively bunch. Words and letters shuffle, twist, and turn in all sorts of directions to make life difficult for the code breakers. Letters disguise themselves by pretending they're other letters. *A*, for example, might masquerade as *B* or *K* or *Q*—or all three of these letters at once. Making and breaking such codes takes a quick wit, patience, and keen detective work.

Another point is worth mentioning. When you send a secret message to a friend in your code club, we say he *decodes* it, because he has the key to unlock its secret. The "enemy" *cryptanalyzes* or *breaks* your code by sheer skill and patience, without any help from you. You'll notice, too, that "enemy" always comes dressed up in quotes when it appears in this book. It means a "friendly enemy"—your sister or brother, or a member of a rival code club who likes to snoop around, trying his skill at breaking your codes as often as you turn them out.

In the introduction to any book, I'm sure that the author is tempted to tell the reader that he is in for a great treat; that *this* book is "neat," "cool," "super," or whatever the current word for wonderful happens to be.

Yet, this is a temptation he should avoid. A book speaks for itself. If it is clear and honest and full of life, the reader will know without being told. Such books, I think, are among the best friends we can have.

I hope this is the way you will feel about *All Kinds of Codes*.

Walt Babson

Easy- and Tough-to-Break Substitution Codes

WHEN JULIUS CAESAR wasn't busy running the Roman Empire he used to try his hand at code making. One of his favorites is still hanging around. As you might guess, it's called Caesar's code. And though it's better than nothing, it's not much better.

All he did was replace the regular letters of the alphabet with letters standing three places further down the line. *A* became *D*, *B* became *E*, *C* became *F* and so on.

Take a look at the alphabets below and you'll see better what I mean.

A B C D E F G H I J K L M N O P Q R S T U V W X Y Z
D E F G H I J K L M N O P Q R S T U V W X Y Z A B C

The top line of letters is our regular alphabet. Beneath it are the letters that Caesar substituted for them.

So when Caesar sent the message *Attack at dawn,* it came out *Dwwdfn dw gdzq.* It reads like alphabet soup, yet anyone who knows codes would break it open quickly. But hold on to the *idea* behind it, because I'm coming back to it right away to give it a new twist.

AUGUSTUS'S CODE

Caesar's nephew Augustus wasn't quite the man his uncle was, and his code was even simpler than Caesar's. How he ever got it by the enemy is one of history's puzzles—but he did. Augustus just substituted the next letter of the alphabet for the original one. *A* became *B, B* became *C,* and so on right to the end of the line, where Z became *A.*

Look at the alphabets below and you'll see how it works.

A B C D E F G H I J K L M N O P Q R S T U V W X Y Z
B C D E F G H I J K L M N O P Q R S T U V W X Y Z A

The bottom letters are the ones Augustus substituted for those of the regular alphabet above it.

So, in Augustus's code, *Attack at dawn* ended up as

Buubdl bu ebxo. Mysterious looking, yes. But don't use it unless you want the world to know your secrets.

KEY-NUMBER CODE

For this type of code you choose a number like 31 or 45 or 57 or whatever. Suppose you want to code *Attack at dawn.* You and your pal decide to use 31 as your key number.

What this number means is that the first letter of your message is written *three* letters higher in the alphabet— the way Caesar's was. The second letter of your message is written *one* letter higher in the alphabet—the way Augustus's was. You follow this pattern until *Attack at dawn* ends up as *Duwbfl du gbzo.*

What I've done is combine the weak codes of Caesar and Augustus and come up with one that's not easy to crack.

KEY-WORD CODES

Here's a nifty little substitution code that's speedy to write and fairly tough to untangle. Just think of a word of five or more letters in which *no letter is used more than once.* Let's say it's *scout.* Write it down, then follow it with the letters of the alphabet that *are not* in the key word, as you see here:

S C O U T A B D E F G H I

J K L M N P Q R V W X Y Z

You'll notice that there are thirteen letters on the top line and thirteen letters on the line below it. When coding your message, just use the letter *above* or *below* the actual letter in your message.

Take the message *Meet me after school* and let's see how it comes out. *M* is the first letter you want to encode. The letter above it is *U*. *E* is the second letter you want to encode. The letter below it is *V*. Follow this route and your coded message reads: *Uvvn uv pwnvd jkyllo.* To make it really snoop-proof, break up the letters into any size words you want, like this: *Uvv nuv pwnv djk yllo.*

Another way of doing a key-word code is to write out the alphabet from *A* to *Z* and under it write a key word and the remaining letters of the alphabet. Since *key word* has no repeated letters, let's use it.

A B C D E F G H I J K L M N O P Q R S T U V W X Y Z

K E Y W O R D A B C F G H I J L M N P Q S T U V X Z

Now, *Meet me after school* becomes *Hooq ho krgon pyajjg.* This is a bit more difficult for the "enemy" to break than the first key-word code, but it takes you more time to set in code. So take your choice.

CRISSCROSS CODE

Caesar never thought of this code, but the *idea* behind it was like his. Here, instead of substituting one letter for one other, it can be substituted for a great number of letters. Anyone who tries to pry open the secret of this code is guaranteed to go right up a wall.

Take a look at the box below.

	AB	**CD**	**EF**	**GH**	**IJZ**	
	A	B	C	D	E	**KLM**
	F	G	H	I	J	**NOP**
	K	L	M	N	O	**QRS**
	P	Q	R	S	T	**TUV**
	U	V	W	X	Y-Z	**WXY**

You see that the boxed letters of the alphabet run five across and five deep, with Y *or* Z in the lower right-hand box. Above them and to the right of them, run other combinations of boldface letters.

Let's take the letter *A*. It can be changed into any one of a dozen two-letter combinations. Since **AB** is above it and **KLM** to the far right of it, using one letter from each group, *A* can become: AK, AL, AM, KA, LA, MA, BK, BL, BM, KB, LB, or MB. Take your choice!

The letter *O* (as well as the other letters in the vertical column at the far right) has even more possibilities, since it has **IJZ** above it, and **QRS** to the right of it. It can be changed into eighteen two-letter combinations: IQ, IR, IS, QI, RI, SI, JQ, JR, JS, QJ, RJ, SJ, ZQ, ZR, ZS, QZ, RZ, or SZ.

The message *Meet me at noon* can be coded in more

ways than any of us would like to count. But here's one way: *Erilmjuj fsjl lbvi shjrqiqg.*

You can make the code even tougher to crack by running all the letters together. But then you must remember to use a double letter as a space between words. The message above would then be: *Erilmjujfffsjlpplbviaashjrqiqg.* Notice that the letters I plugged in were *ff, pp,* and *aa.* Now the message looks like something that could have come out of King Tut's tomb—and perhaps ought to be put back.

BACON'S ABC CODE

Francis Bacon was quite a man, with a stack of titles to prove it—"Sir," "Baron," "Viscount"—and best of all, "Lord" Chancellor of England. Bacon lived about 350 years ago, when King James I ruled England.

But the king didn't hand out titles for nothing. He knew that Francis Bacon was a statesman, a gifted writer, and a philosopher. In short, Bacon was a thinker, who used his brain to find out the why and how of things.

Like so many famous men, he was also a gifted code maker. His rules for code making are still the best of all:

1. That it be not laborious to write and read.
2. That it be impossible to decipher.
3. That, in some cases, it be without suspicion.

At the time he made up the code I'm going to show you, it seemed foolproof. But today, a cryptanalyst— or code detective—could break it easily. Yet, simple as it looks, it's likely to stump your friends.

This is the key to Bacon's system:

	AA	BB	CC	AB	AC	BC	CB	CA
A	a	b	c	d	e	f	g	h
B	i	j-k	l	m	n	o	p	q
C	r	s	t	u	v	w	x	y-z

Suppose you wanted to send this message: *I think you're swell.* Look for the *i* in the box. To the left of it is the capital letter B. Above it is the letter combination AA. So—*i* becomes BAA. The letter *t* has the capital letter C to the left of it, and the combination CC above it. It becomes CCC. From there on, use this method to encode your message. You'll also notice that *j* and *k* have the same code letters, BBB, as do *y* and *z* (CCA).

Here is how *I think you're swell* turns out in code: BAA, CCC, ACA, BAA, BAC, BBB, CCA, BBC, CAB, CAA, AAC, CBB, CBC, AAC, BCC, BCC.

To fool any hot code breaker, get rid of the commas, or replace them with any letters of the alphabet that come to mind—except A, B or C. Then you'll come up with something like this: BAAGCCCNACADBAARBAC KBBBZCCANBBCVCABLCAAQAACRCBBOCBCKA ACSBCCTBCC. And that's quite a mess of message to untangle—unless you know the key to it.

If you'd like to save space, and make this code even more confusing than before, try this:

Let A equal   \   a line slanted to the left

Let B equal | a vertical line

Let C equal   /   a line slanted to the right

In this way, for instance, the word *dog* becomes \\| |/ \\/| standing for AAB, BBC, ACB

PRISONER'S CODE

During the early 1800s, Czar Nicholas I of Russia stayed in power by keeping his foot on everybody's neck. One way he did this was to hire men who were top-notch code breakers, or cryptanalysts. He would station them in post offices all over Russia to poke through people's mail to see if they were hatching any plots against the czar. If they were, they ended up in a stone dungeon, with nobody to keep them company.

It wasn't long before the prisoners were crowded with people who hated the czar and his code breakers. So to stay sane—and swap escape plans—the prisoners made up a tapping code that enabled them to "talk" to each other.

Luckily, you don't have to be in prison to try it out, so let's look at how it works.

First of all, the letters of the alphabet are divided into

a checkerboard pattern, as you see below, with numbers running down the left side and across the top of them.

	1	2	3	4	5
1	A	B	C	D	E
2	F	G	H	I or J	K
3	L	M	N	O	P
4	Q	R	S	T	U
5	V	W	X	Y	Z

Suppose you wanted to tap out "Hello" to a fellow sufferer. First you found the letter H on your checkerboard. To the left of it was the number 2. Above it was the number 3. So you *tapped twice,* paused, and *tapped three times.* That zeroed your friend in on the letter H—located in the second *horizontal* row and the third *vertical* row.

E had the number 1 to the left of it, and the number 5 above it. So you *tapped once,* paused, then *tapped five times.*

L had the number 3 to the left of it, and the number 1

above it. So you tapped *three times,* paused, and *tapped once.* The next L was tapped out in the same way.

Then the letter O—with number 3 to the left of it and number 4 above it—was *three taps,* pause, *four taps.*

Since the prisoners didn't have much else to do, they memorized the code and could "talk" to each other at about 15 words a minute.

If you're lucky enough to have a brother or sister around the house, you can tap out messages to each other at night on your bedroom walls. Or if you're a Scout, you and your patrol buddies can blink secret messages from tent to tent with your flashlights. You can't send it as fast as Morse Code—but it's a lot quicker to learn. Besides, Scouts don't use the Morse Code much any more.

During the day you can send it by waving your arms. For instance, left arm out *three times,* right arm out *twice,* would be *M.*

The prisoner's code can also be written. It's a simple substitution code—with one difference: numbers are substituted for letters, instead of letters for letters.

Can you figure out this message: 32151544321531144 1542? Well, the first number is 3, the second 2. The letter in your prisoner's square with the 3 to the left of it and the 2 above it is *M.* The next two numbers are 1 and 5. The letter with the 1 to the left of it and the 5 above it is *E.* If you go along in this way, finding out which letter each two numbers stand for, your message will come out: MEET ME LATER.

If you have a typewriter around your house, here's another way of sending the Prisoner's Code. In the box below, just substitute a *comma* for 1, a *semicolon* for 2, a *colon* for 3, a *period* for 4, and an *apostrophe* for 5.

$$1 =, \quad 2 =; \quad 3 =: \quad 4 =. \quad 5 ='$$

1 = ,	A	B	C	D	E
2 = ;	F	G	H	I-J	K
3 = :	L	M	N	O	P
4 = .	Q	R	S	T	U
5 = '	V	W	X	Y	Z

Now, the message *Meet me later* comes out :;,',',..:;,':,,, ..,'.; Even a supersnoop would have a tough time with that, typed or written.

No Russians hated the czar more than a group of revolutionaries called the Nihilists. Until they came up with the baffling code we're going to examine next, they often used invisible ink messages in their plots against his life. They'd dissolve sugar in water, dip a pen into it, then write a message. In a few seconds the "ink" dried up and disappeared from sight. (Sometimes they used saliva.) When a fellow Nihilist got the message, which was often written in the blank places of an ordinary letter, he'd heat the paper with a match and the message reappeared.

When the czar's men got wind of this, they started heating—and breaking—many of the Nihilists' messages. But the Nihilists had the last, cruel laugh. They sent one final batch of "invisible" messages that they knew would be intercepted soaked beforehand in a solution of gun cotton, an explosive. When the czar's men put a flame to them, the letters blew up in their faces.

When the smoke cleared, the Nihilists came up with another dirty trick—the ingenious code you're about to see.

THE NIHILIST NUMBER CODE

All during the 1800s the Nihilists were plotting to plant a bomb under the czar, no matter which one was in power at the time—Nicholas I, Alexander II or Alexander III. They thought that if he were out of the way, the country would run the way they wanted it to. They hated the czar and everything he stood for—the Russian government, its culture and its religion.

Of course the czar was out to get them because he didn't take kindly to people who wanted to blow him up. So the Nihilists, just to stay alive and continue their plots against him, devised many secret codes. The best of them was the Nihilist Number Code.

The men who originated it used the very same letter-number arrangement used in the Prisoner's Code:

	1	2	3	4	5
1	A	B	C	D	E
2	F	G	H	I-J	K
3	L	M	N	O	P
4	Q	R	S	T	U
5	V	W	X	Y	Z

Now, with an ingenious twist, they made the fairly simple Prisoner's Code a hundred times more difficult to break. When they wanted to code a message, they first chose a key word that they wrote under the message. Let's use the word CAT, though the length of the key word doesn't much matter. Suppose the message was *Down with the Czar*. They would write it out in this way with the key word repeated underneath it:

Message: *Down   with   the   Czar*
Key word: CATC ATCA TCA TCAT

Then they did some simple addition. The first letter of the message to be coded is *D*. In the square, *D* equals 14. The key-word letter C, beneath it, equals 13. When they added the two together they came up with the number 27—the first number of the coded message.

The second letter of the message was *o*. It equaled 34 in the square. The key-word letter A, beneath it, equaled 11. Together they added up to 45—the second number in the coded message.

Following this system of adding *w* to T, *n* to C, *w* to A, etc.—this was their final coded message:

27 45 96 46 63 68 57 34 88 36 26 57 68 22 86

Such messages were quick and easy to send, and stumped the czar's code breakers.

When the other Nihilist received this coded message, he knew that *his* key word was CAT. (No more than two Nihilists ever used the same key word.) So he merely subtracted C, that equaled 13, from code number 27, and came up with 14. Number 14 in the square is the letter *D*—the first letter of the original message.

Then he subtracted A, that equaled 11 in the square, from code number 45, and came up with 34. Number 34 in the square is the letter *o*—the second letter of the original message.

Going along in this way—subtracting T from 96, C from 46, A from 63, T from 68, etc.—he uncovered the hidden message.

You might wonder if the Nihilists' plots to bomb the czar ever came to pass. The answer is yes, for Czar Alexander II, a decent man who had made many social reforms, was killed in 1881 by a bomb as he rode down a street in St. Petersburg.

Up, Down and All Around Codes

IN ENGLISH we write from the left side of the paper to the right side. And many of us think that everyone else writes in the same way, but that's not always so. The Arabs write from the right to the left. The Chinese write from the right side of the page up.

Since code makers are clever people, they're always making up codes based on the idea that you can write in all sorts of directions and fool the code breakers.

To see how these codes work, write out a message in a 36-letter square like the one below. Let's say it's *I will meet you at dawn tomorrow at my house*. The X at the end is called a *null*—a letter stuck in to fill out the square.

I W I L L M→
E E T Y O U→
A T D A W N→
T O M O R R→
O W A T M Y→
H O U S E X→

If you left your message in this form, even a tenth-rate code breaker would be in on your secret. So let's see how we can stump him or her.

CHINESE CODE

You'll remember that the Chinese write from the right side of the page up. So all we do with our message is this:

I W I L L M
E E T Y O U
A T D A W N
T O M O R R
O W A T M Y
H O U S E X

Just follow the arrows, and your message becomes *xyrnum emrwol stoayl uamdti owotew hotaei.*

The next thing you have to do is tip off your secret agent pal which code you're using. Try something sly like *Confucius says: xyrnum emrwol stoayl uamdti owotew hotaei.* Or maybe just write the name of a Chinese city like Peking or Hong Kong in front of your message.

Now that he has the key that this is the Chinese Code,
all he does is write the first word of your message—*xyrnum*
—*up* in this way:

m

u

n

r

y

x

Then the second word, *emrwol* goes to the left of it, like
this:

l m

o u

w n

r r

m y

e x

Continue on, until your message shows up like this:

~~i w i l l m~~►

~~e e t y o u~~►

~~a t d a w n~~►

~~t o m o r r~~►

~~o w a t m y~~►

~~h o u s e x~~►

ARAB CODE

Since Arabs write from right to left, here's how the
same message would come out in Arabian code:

A slick word you might use to tip your friend off on this code is *oil*—something the Arabs have plenty of. Then our message would read: *Oil: Mlliwi uoytee nwadta rromot ymtawo xesuoh.* To decode it is a cinch. Starting with the first word in your message, your friend reads each one backwards. *Mlliwi* becomes *iwillM, uoytee* becomes *eetyou*—and so on—until it comes out *iwillMeet youatdawnatmyhousex.*

There are all sorts of other tricky codes you can make up in this way. How about a **Spaghetti Code?**

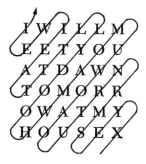

In code—starting at the bottom right letter—it is *xyesmr nrtuoa owumoa mwhood yllttt aeiwei.* All your friend has to do to decode your message is draw a square with 36 boxes in it and run the spaghetti line through it. Then he puts the first letter of your message—*x*—in the lower right hand box. The *y*, your second message letter, goes above the *x*, and so on, along the spaghetti trail. The diagram below shows how the decoder would get started.

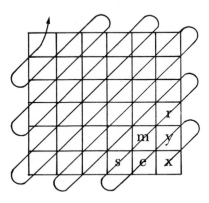

Now for some other codes that we can call

The Corkscrew Code

The Rainstorm Code

The Farmer's Plow Path Code

Take your choice!

RAIL FENCE CODE

This code has been around almost as long as fences. It's quick to write and not so easy to untangle—unless you know how.

Suppose you want to send the message LOUIS LIKES BEAN SOUP. Just drop every second letter down—

in a rail fence pattern. Then take the bottom line of letters and put them next to the top line of letters and you'll come up with: LUSIEBASU OILKSENOP. If you'd like to make it even more confusing, just break the letters up in any old way you want, like: LUSIE BASUO ILK SENOP.

When your code club friend wants to find out what message is hidden in this strange-sounding mass of letters, he just counts the number of letters in the message. This one has 18 letters, so he takes the last nine—OILK SENOP—and puts them back under the first nine, like this:

Then he reads down, the way the arrows point, and comes up with your message—*Louis likes bean soup.*

If your message has an *odd* number of letters, as in *Hello John*, you encode it the same way as we did the message above:

It then comes out HLOON ELJH. Maybe, to make it more confusing, you decide to break it up into H LOON ELJH.

This time, when your friend decodes it, he finds that the secret message has an *odd* number of letters. This one has nine letters, so he takes the first five and under them writes the last four letters, like this:

Then he reads the message by following the arrows.

BROKEN-WORD CODE

Do you see the message hidden here? IN EE DH EL PN OW.

It's there, like the nose on your face. But the reason you might have missed uncovering it is that most of us tend to concentrate on the two-letter combinations instead of piecing them together into words and sentences. It says: *I need help now.*

THE SWINGING SQUARE CODE

Suppose you took the word *codes* and shuffled the letters around until they came out *desoc.* You'd be taking a word that makes sense and changing it into a *nonsense* word. (It's hard to believe, but a five-letter word like *codes* can be changed into 119 other such "words".) At any rate, this shuffling of letters to mask a word's identity is the idea behind all *transposition* codes.

So far every code we've looked at in this chapter has been a *transposition* code. Here's another, with a new twist to it. It was dreamed up by the Germans during World War I, and it took French code breakers four months before they were able to crack it.

It's a little-known code, quick to write, and just as quick to decode—if you have the key.

First of all, make an exact duplicate of the diagram you see below. Do this by laying a piece of writing paper over it and tracing through it. Cut out your large square and then cut out all nine blank squares just as they are in the drawing.

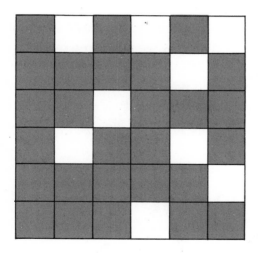

Now you have the key to writing *and* decoding a message of thirty-six letters or less.

Just place your cutout on a piece of blank paper. Then, progressing from left to right, top to bottom, fill in the blank squares with the first nine letters of your message, as you see on page 26. (And don't forget to make pencil marks where your square touches the paper.)

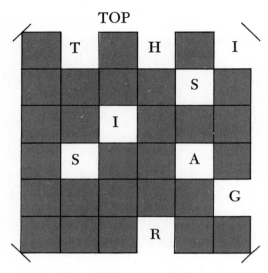

Now, since your cutout is the key to this puzzle, let's do what we all do when we put a key in a lock—*turn the key to the right*. In other words, rotate your cutout so that the three open windows that were across the top are now running down the right side. Then fill in the next nine letters of your message, as you see below.

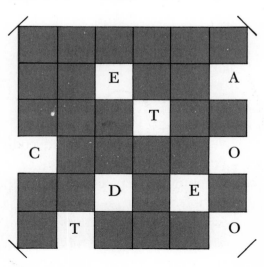

From here on in it's a cinch—one more turn to the right for another piece of your message—

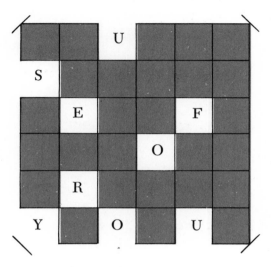

and then the last quarter turn to the right completes your 36-letter message: **THIS IS A GREAT CODE TO USE FOR YOUR CODE CLUB.**

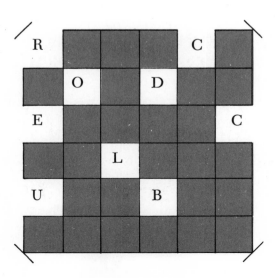

Now, when you lift your cutout off the sheet of paper you've been writing on, this is what you'll see:

R	T	U	H	C	I
S	O	E	D	S	A
E	E	I	T	F	C
C	S	L	O	A	O
U	R	D	B	E	G
Y	T	O	R	U	O

When you send this message to your friend, who has a duplicate of your cutout, he just puts his cutout over this square of letters. The first nine letters of your message—THISISAGR—will appear. He'll then give it a turn to the right, and EATCODETO will appear. Two more such turns and he'll have your complete message: THIS IS A GREAT CODE TO USE FOR YOUR CODE CLUB.

You and your friend must also remember which side of your cutouts you'll use for the top, or starting position when you encode and decode your messages.

This is also a first-class code to use in your diary or logbook if you have some private thoughts you want to write down.

These cutouts, or grilles, can be made with as many squares as you want. The most useful sizes are 6 by 6, 8 by 8, and 10 by 10. The diagrams below show you usable ones in each of these sizes.

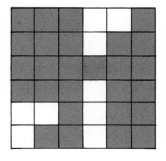
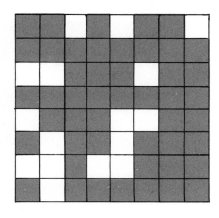

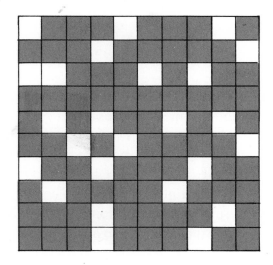

In a 6-by-6 square you can write a 36-letter message. In an 8-by-8 square you can write a 64-letter message.

And in a 10-by-10 square you can write a hundred-letter message. If any of your messages run short, just fill in the blank spaces with nulls—any letters that come to mind.

If you'd like to make up your own grille, with the openings arranged differently from any you see on this page, this is how you do it. I'll use a 6-by-6 as an example, but the same system will work with bigger or smaller grilles.

1	2	3	4	5	1
5	6	7	8	6	2
4	8	9	9	7	3
3	7	9	9	8	4
2	6	8	7	6	5
1	5	4	3	2	1

Number the little squares as you see. Then cut out one of the number 1 cells. Next, cut out one of the number 2 cells. Do this until you've cut out one of each of the numbers. That means that you'll have nine open spaces. When you finish turning your cutout, you'll find that these 9 open spaces cover all 36 of the boxes.

One more security tip. To really baffle anyone who might get hold of your cutout, don't write your message left to right, top to bottom, as the code breaker might expect. Instead, fill in the squares from bottom to top, right to left, the way we did with our Chinese Code. Or maybe try the Arab Code—right to left, top to bottom. Or better yet, try the Farmer's Plow Path route—up on the far right column, down on the next, and so on.

Take the first cutout I showed you how to make for the Swinging Square Code and see if you're sharp enough to find out if I've used the Chinese, Arab, or Farmer's Plow route with this message. Hint: Ding, dong, bell. . . .

/ G E E S M H \

D N R S I R

Z O T E O A

L H I M S A

Z H S U M T

\ I P T I W F /

SWISS CHEESE GRILLE

This grille doesn't do any swinging. But it's a corker for sending a scrambled message that's darn near impossible to figure out. And you can zip out a message in wink-quick time.

A Scout in my troop invented it, tried it out on me, and stumped me with it. And nobody else in our troop could figure it out either.

So, in honor of the inventor, let's rename it the *Louie Schmidt Swiss Cheese Grille*. It's really something to chew on.

To make it, you'll need a piece of paper about three inches square, with thirty-six small squares inside it. Make one, then trace a second one from the first. Lay the squares on top of each other, and, with a paper punch, poke holes in the center of each of the squares. Now you'll have duplicate grilles—one for you, and one for your code club pal.

The black circles in the diagram below are the punched-out holes. You'll also notice curved marks below and above some of the punch holes. Mark them on your grilles just as you see them in the diagram.

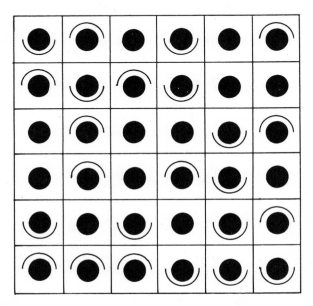

Now, to write your coded message, lay your grille on a blank piece of paper. Suppose you want to scramble the message WHAT CAME FIRST, THE CHICKEN OR THE EGG? Starting with the upper left-hand box with the ⌣ mark on it, fill in the first twelve letters of your message—left to right—in all the punch holes marked ⌣.

Then fill the next nine letters in all the holes marked ⌢. Last, fill in all the remaining, unmarked holes with the rest of your secret message.

When you've done that, here's what your message will look like:

W	T	R	H	T	T
H	A	E	T	H	E
E	C	G	G	C	H
?	I	Z	C	A	Z
M	X	E	Y	F	K
E	N	O	I	R	S

When your friend gets it, he puts his Swiss Cheese Grille over it and reads the letters showing over the ∪ marks. Then he reads the letters showing under the ∩ marks. Last, he reads the letters showing in the unmarked punch holes.

And out will jump your message, like a rabbit out of a bush.

WHAT
CAME
FIRST
THE
CHICKEN
OR THE
EGG?
ZZXY

THE DIRTY TRICKS CODE

The 1876 presidential election was the only one in
American history in which the man with the most popular votes lost the election. The loser, Democrat Samuel
Tilden, got 4,285,992 votes—about 250,000 more than
his Republican opponent Rutherford B. Hayes. But elec-
toral votes from each state are what really count, and
Hayes ended up with 185 to Tilden's 184. The Democrats
then accused the Republicans of buying the electors'
votes in a few of the states. That got the Republicans
sore, so they found, and broke, coded telegrams that the
Democrats had sent to some electors—and proved that
it was the Democrats who were trying to buy the votes.

This was a sad time for Americans when they learned
that not everyone in high office is honorable. Justice tri-
umphed for a time, and the few Democrats involved got
kicked out of politics. Since they were shady characters
anyway, their only regret was that they hadn't made up
a break-proof code and saved their skins.

Actually, the code was a pretty good one that took
some first-class code breakers months to figure out.

This is how it works:

                                   1   2   3   4   5
Let's take an elephant joke: What do you know when
 6   7   8   9   10   11 12 13   14
you see three elephants walking down the street wearing
  15   16   17   18 19 20 21   22
pink sweatshirts? They're all on the same team!

Notice that I put numbers over each of the words, from
1 to 22. If the words stay in that order, they make sense.

Move them around, and they don't make sense. So let's

scramble all twenty-two numbers like this:
$$\overset{5}{when} \quad \overset{4}{know}$$
$$\overset{3}{you} \, \overset{8}{three} \, \overset{10}{walking} \, \overset{9}{elephants} \, \overset{1}{what} \, \overset{2}{do} \, \overset{7}{see} \, \overset{6}{you} \, \overset{15}{pink} \, \overset{14}{wearing}$$
$$\overset{13}{street} \, \overset{18}{all} \, \overset{20}{the} \, \overset{19}{on} \, \overset{11}{down} \, \overset{12}{the} \, \overset{17}{they're} \, \overset{16}{sweatshirts} \, \overset{21}{same} \, \overset{22}{team}$$

I've now shown you just *one* way to jumble the twenty-two-word elephant joke. An amazing fact about it is that it can be rearranged in 281,000,000,000,000,000,000 (two hundred and eighty-one quintillion) different ways. And even an elephant will tell you, two hundred and eighty-one quintillion makes a million look like peanuts! Yet this code was broken by amateur cryptanalysts, using a method that's called *multiple anagramming*. But don't be frightened off by the words. I'll show you how anagramming works in our *Tips for Code Breakers* chapter.

Two questions remain to be answered: What's the quickest way for you to encode this type of message? What's the easiest way for your friends to decode it?

Here's how. Think of a ten-letter key word or phrase *with no duplicate letters.* Share this word with your code club friends. We'll try PRECAUTION. Now, rearrange it in alphabetical order and it becomes ACEINOPRTU.

To encode your message, write it out *under* the letters of PRECAUTION as you see here.

P	R	E	C	A	U	T	I	O	N
vhat	do	you	know	when	you	see	three	elephants	walking
down	the	street	wearing	pink	sweatshirts	they're	all	on	the
ame	team								

Now all you do is write ACEINOPRTU across a piece of paper and under **A** the words *when, pink;* under **C** the words *know, wearing,* and so forth—as you see below:

A	C	E	I	N	O	P	R	T	U
when	know	you	three	walking	elephants	what	do	see	you
pink	wearing	street	all	the	on	down	the	they're	sweatshirts
						same	team		

When the "enemy" sees this message: *when know you three walking elephants what do see you pink wearing street all the on down the they're sweatshirts same team* —he'll have a hard time making sense of it unless he knows multiple anagramming. But your code club friends will have no difficulty decoding the message because they know the key word is PRECAUTION. So they write the alphabetical version of it—ACEINOPRTU—across a sheet of paper, and under each letter they write the words of your coded message, like this:

A	C	E	I	N	O	P	R	T	U
when	know	you	three	walking	elephants	what	do	see	you
pink	wearing	street	all	the	on	down	the	they're	sweatshirts
						same	team		

Then they merely rearrange the columns under ACEINOPRTU into the key word PRECAUTION, and earn a laugh for their work:

P	R	E	C	A	U	T	I	O	N
What	do	you	know	when	you	see	three	elephants	walking
down	the	street	wearing	pink	sweatshirts	they're	all	on	the
same	team								

Using this system, you can write a code message of any length. Remember, though, that the longer the message is, the more difficult it becomes to break. You can also add to the code breaker's problems by removing capital letters, commas, and periods from the coded message.

Old
and New
Position
Codes

I DON'T KNOW if you've ever thought of it this way, but our alphabet is one of the most important families we have. As families go, it's a big one, with twenty-six members. Their job is to get together to make words and sentences so that all of us can understand each other when we write or talk.

But code makers aren't happy when *everyone* knows what's going on. They like to share secrets with a few of their friends and gum up the works for the rest of us.

So, in the hands of code makers, our letters do strange things. They stand on their heads ⊥ , or stretch out on their stomachs **ᗡ** , or lie down on their backs **ᙏ** . When we see them this way they're hard to recognize. Their *position* is what fools us.

THE FLIP-FLOP CODE

Say you wanted to set this sentence in Flip-Flop Code:

MEET ME AT NOON

First, you'd print an *M*. Then you'd slide your writing paper a quarter turn clockwise, stop, and put in the second letter of your message: *E*. Then another quarter turn, stop, and add the third letter: *E*. Continue this way and your final encoded message would look like this:

MШƎ⊣ІMШⱯ⊣NOOZ

Now let's try a more mysterious version, with the same basic idea.

m ᘐ ᘔ ⱨ m ᘙ ᙁ ⱨ ᙁ ᕷ ᕴ ᕶ

Yes, it's the very same message: MEET ME AT NOON. But this time we've substituted *script* or *cursive* letters for the *block* or *printed* ones. Try turning it around, quarter turn by quarter turn, and each letter will show up bright and clear.

Still, we're not quite finished with the possibilities of the Flip-Flop. Let's write the same message so that it reads from right to left—Arab style. Another thing. The letter *O* is a high frequency letter, which means that it

shows up in words very often—far more, for instance,
than Z or K or L and many others. And, since *O* looks
pretty much the same right side up, or sideways, or up-
side down, it could provide a valuable clue to someone
who wants to break the code. So, now and then, replace
it with a dot.

If we add these twists to the Flip-Flop Code, here's
how *Meet me at noon* will finally appear in its most diffi-
cult-to-break form.

$$\bar{z}\,{}^{\bullet}.\,\mathcal{n}\,\dagger\,\mathcal{v}\,\mathfrak{q}\,\mathcal{m}\,\dagger\,\mathcal{v}\,\mathfrak{q}\,\mathcal{m}$$

You'll remember that in our first two chapters we
talked about *substitution* codes and *transposition* codes.
Position codes are a mix of both of these. In the Flip-Flop
we've just covered, every letter of the alphabet was substituted for *itself*—not some other letter or number. But
each of these letters was also transposed, or turned
around, so the Flip-Flop was a transposition code, too.

THE DOT CODE

In the next position code we're going to look at, *all* of
the letters of our alphabet will be substituted for dots!
Where the dots are placed, or positioned, is the key to
an old, but still puzzling code.

For writing the Dot Code it's best to use lined paper.
On the top line I've written a mixed-up alphabet, with the
letters evenly spaced across the sheet, as you see. (Can
you figure out the message? It's something you're going
to do right now.)

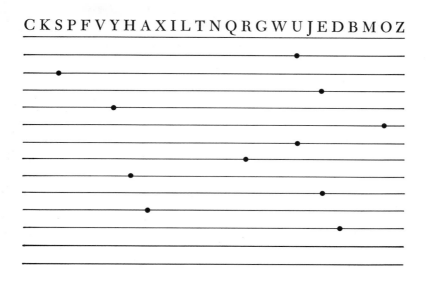

C K S P F V Y H A X I L T N Q R G W U J E D B M O Z

In case you couldn't uncover the message, here's how you go about it. Find the *highest* dot on the paper. It's on the line nearest the alphabet, under the letter *U*. The next highest dot is under the letter *S*, and so on down. The complete message reads: *Use your head.*

If you have a sheet or two of lined paper handy, make up a mixed-up alphabet of your own—with copies for one or two of your friends. Write out the alphabet across the top line of the paper the way I've shown you, and then cut it off with a pair of scissors.

To encode your message, slide your alphabet down to the top line of your paper, mark a dot under the first letter of your message, then slide the alphabet down to the next line and make a dot under the second letter of your message, and so on.

When your friend gets the message, he simply slides his duplicate alphabet down the sheet of paper the same way you did, until he touches the first dot, the second dot, the third dot, and so on, decoding the message as he goes along.

Decoding the message in this way is easy because your friend has the key to it. But woe to anyone without the alphabet key who tries to make sense out of that mess of dots. They'll drive the person dotty—because there's just no way to read even that short a message without the key.

After what I've just said, don't think that the Dot Code is 100 percent break-proof. It isn't, because for every code maker there seems to be an equally clever code breaker, or cryptanalyst, sniffing out a solution. So if a very clever "enemy" got hold of many different messages you'd written in Dot Code, he *could* pry open your secret alphabet key. How he'd go about doing this is something we'll save for our chapter on *Tips for Code Breakers*.

THE PIGPEN CODE

The symbol ⧉ has played an active part in codes for hundreds of years. It's the basis for what we call the Pigpen Code, so named because when you put letters in the structure, like this—

A	B	C
D	E	F
G	H	I

they're separated from each other by lines, the way pigs are in a pigpen.

During the early 1800s a society that called itself the Free and Accepted Masons began using this code in their secret writings and ceremonies, and they still do. So it's also called the Mason's Code.

You can learn it in a minute or two. Once you get the hang of it, you can memorize it and write it about as quickly as any code I know. Though it's fairly well known, it can still fool most of the people most of the time.

Take a look at the symbols and letters below. You'll notice that there's living space for all 26 letters of our alphabet, with each "room" or "pen" different from the others.

A	B	C		J.	K.	L.		\\ S /		\\ W /
D	E	F		M.	N.	O.		T X U		X· X ·Z
G	H	I		P.	Q.	R.		/ V \\		/ Y \\

Suppose you wanted to set the letter *E* in code. You'll see that *E* lives in a four-walled room: ☐ . *H* lives in a three-walled room: ⊓ . *N* lives in a four-walled room with a dot in it: ☐ . *S* has a two-walled room: ∨ . *Z* has two walls with a dot ⟨ in it.

Get the idea? You merely substitute the shape of the letter's "room" for the letter you wish to encode.

Now, in Pigpen Code, we'll answer the riddle: "What grows up as it grows down?" (Hint—The answer will "quack" you up!)

Since the Pigpen is a straight substitution code, how come it's included in this chapter on position codes? The answer is that the *idea* behind the Pigpen is good enough to borrow. Just add a dash of *transposition* code to it, and it becomes much more difficult to break. In its new form it's called the Tic-Tac-Toe Code.

THE TIC-TAC-TOE CODE

Take a look at the tic-tac-toe symbol below and you'll see that the entire alphabet is contained in its nine different spaces or "rooms," with a question mark added to the right of the letter Z.

ABC	DEF	GHI
JKL	MNO	PQR
STU	VWX	YZ?

Here, again, the shape of each "room" is different from each of the others. Let's concentrate on this space ⌐ on the tic-tac-toe emblem. How would you know whether it stood for A, B, or C? Easy. When it has a dot at the left side of it ⌐ the dot is substituted for A, because A is in the left position. When the dot appears in the middle position ⌐ it's B, because B occupies the middle spot. And this ⌐ would represent C, because C stands at the right side of the space.

As an example, this is how we would encode the word *cab:* ⌐ · ⌐ · ⌐

The very same method of replacing letters with dots is used in each of the nine "rooms." M, for instance, would be ⊡ X would be ⌐· S would be ·⌐ Get the idea?

Using this system, the word *happy* would be:

$$\mathsf{L} \cdot \, \cdot \mathsf{J} \, \boxdot \, \boxdot \, \mathsf{F}$$

It's a tricky code, but an experienced code breaker might not have too much trouble figuring it out, so we'll add a gimmick to tighten it up. Remember the question mark in the lower right hand space? We indicate it with this symbol ⌐· , which means "Stop. Instead of using this lettering system

ABC	DEF	GHI
JKL	MNO	PQR
STU	VWX	YZ?

switch to this one, beginning with the letter B instead of the letter A."

BCD	EFG	HIJ
KLM	NOP	QRS
TUV	WXY	ZA?

Now the word *cab* would be   ⌐· ⌐· ·⌐   instead
of   ·⌐ ·⌐ ·⌐   as it was originally.

What this means is that each letter now has two disguises instead of one, which makes breaking this code
far more difficult than before.

So, when you're encoding a message, each time you decide to use this symbol ⌐· it signals your code club
friends to switch from one alphabet system to the other.
To see if you've got the idea, try to decode this message:

It's M E (shift) E T M E (shift) A T N O (shift) O N
—which spells out MEET ME AT NOON.

If you think all this is pretty shifty, you're right. But
code breakers are a shifty bunch, too—always trying to
poke their noses into your business. So I guess one good
shift deserves another.

THE DING-A-LING CODE

Just about everyone has a telephone or two in his house
nowadays. Yet, if I asked you to draw a rough sketch of
the numbers and letters that show on a telephone dial, I
bet you'd be stumped. I know I was when someone asked
me to do that. In fact, I drew in the letters *Q* and *Z*—
completely forgetting that they're not even on the phone
dial.

Just to refresh your memory, take a look at these
sketches of a dial phone and a push-button phone.

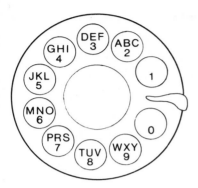
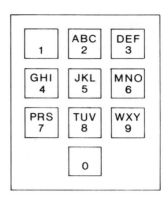

There's a neat little code hidden in these numbers and letters. Basically it's a substitution code, with a pinch of transposition code added, so it rates as a position code.

Notice that the letters over the number 2 are ABC—like this:

Look again, and you'll see that the A is *above* and to the *left* of 2. B is *directly above* 2. And C is *above* and to the *right* of 2.

In our Ding-a-Ling Code, we'll substitute 2 for *A, B,* and *C*. Sound ridiculous? It is, unless we change the position of the 2's like this: 2 ⒉ 2. Now, whether you know it or not, we've just spelled the word *cab* in Ding-a-Ling lingo.

Take another look at those 2's. The first 2 is tilted slightly to the right, at the letter *C*. The second 2 is tilted slightly to the left, at the letter A. The third 2 is standing with its head straight up, pointing at the letter B.

That, in a nutshell, is how the code works. But two letters of the alphabet are missing—Q and Z. Since the numbers 1 and 0 on the phone dial have no letters above them, let 1 stand for Q and 0 stand for Z.

Here are a few sample coded words, just to see that you get the drift of the Ding-a-Ling.

4 3 5 7   is HELP

5 4 6 4   is KING

1 8 4 0   is QUIZ

JARGON CODES

With about a million words in the English language you'd think we'd have more than enough to go around. But we don't seem to. Every day new words spring to life and keep our dictionary makers running around sorting them out and storing them up for us.

If young Abe Lincoln could pay us a short visit, he'd be surprised to find out that he was once a *mouthpiece* (lawyer) who got *bread* (a fee) to keep some *cats* (his clients) out of the *slammer* (jail). Words like *mouthpiece* and such are called jargon, because they mean something special to different groups of people. In a policeman's jargon, or lingo, almost everyone suspected of committing a crime is the "alleged perpetrator." In Hippie jargon, Santa Claus is "the fat cat with the red threads." In baseball jargon, a left-handed pitcher is a "southpaw."

Some people, with time on their hands, have even devised jargon—or secret—languages. Even if you never speak them, it's worthwhile to know how they work, because they're position codes that "talk."

In **Pig Latin** we add WAY to words that begin with a vowel: APE becomes APE'WAY, EGG becomes EGG'WAY, INK becomes INK'WAY, and so on. When a word begins with a *single* consonant followed by one or more vowels, we move the consonant to the end of the word, then add AY. CAT becomes AT'CAY. HORSE becomes ORSE'HAY. BEAN becomes EAN'BAY. And last, when a word begins with *two or more* consonants, they are moved to the end of the word and AY is added. For example: STICK becomes ICK'STAY, THE becomes E'THAY, STRAIGHT becomes AIGHT'STRAY.

O'SAY UCH'MAY OR'FAY IG'PAY ATIN'LAY—let's move on to Tut Latin.

In **King Tut Latin**, we stick TUT between the syllables of words. BUTTER is BUT'TUT'TER. BANANA comes out BA'TUT'NA'TUT'NA—a word that could drive *you* bananas.

Turkey Irish goes like this: Add AB before each vowel in a word. This *seems* simple until you try it. The word ABRACADABRA in Turkey Irish comes out ABAB'-RABA'CABA'DABAB'RABA. Better yet, forget that and try DOG—it comes out DAB'OG.

Speaking **Opish** is as hard as whistling *Yankee Doodle* with a peanut butter sandwich in your mouth. If you're game, stick OP after each consonant in a word. One other thing—when consonants are repeated, like *tt* or *nn*, OP is added after the pair, not between them. In Opish, JOHN SMITH comes up with this bouncy new name: JOP'O'HOP'NOP SOP'MOP'I'TOP'HOP.

Double Dutch looks like the hardest to learn of all these secret languages we've mentioned. Yet, it really isn't. Once you get the hang of it, you can speak it almost as quickly as Pig Latin, and faster than the others you've seen. A friend of mine, who'd learned it as a young girl, rattled it off so fast that I couldn't get one word of what she was saying.

First thing to remember is that all the vowels are pronounced exactly the same as they are in regular English. No problem there.

The consonants, though, are replaced by easy-to-remember, silly-sounding syllables. Here they are:

B	BUB	K	KUK	S	SUS
C	CASH	L	LUL	T	TUT
D	DUD	M	MUM	V	VUV
F	FUF	N	NUN	W	WASH
G	GUG	P	PUP	X	XUX
H	HUTCH	Q	QUACK	Y	YUB
J	JUG	R	RUG	Z	ZUB

When we try JACK AND JILL WENT UP THE HILL it comes out JUG'A'CASH'KUK A'NUN'DUD JUG'I'LUL'LUL WASH'E'NUN'TUT U'PUP TUT' HUTCH'E HUTCH'I'LUL'LUL.

These jargon codes join our family of position codes because they substitute one word for another—DOG equals OGDAY, for instance. And, in order to do this, jargon codes move, or transpose, letters and syllables.

Some people think that secret languages are silly, and that we'd be far better off to learn Latin or Greek or

French. For the most part they're right. Foreign languages *are* valuable to us. They are among the most difficult "codes" to break, and by breaking them we come to know more about the people who share the world with us.

But there's a place for Pig Latin and Double Dutch and Turkey Irish, too. They're fun to try out. They make you laugh. And if you learn to laugh when you're young, you're not likely to forget how later on.

Tips
for
Code Breakers

IN OUR LAST chapter I said that our alphabet is a family that gets together to make up words and sentences. Like many big families, our alphabet has its go-getters, working their heads off—and others who prefer to take life easy.

Consider the letters *e* and *t*, for instance. They're workhorses that show up more than any other letters of our alphabet. If you were to count 400 letters from anything you read you'd probably find that *e* shows up about 52 times and *t* about 36 times, while *z* and *q* will show up once, if at all.

So, to give credit where it's due, we call this ambitious

crowd—*e,t,a,o,n,i,r,s,h*—the *high frequency letters*, because they make up about 70 percent of all our words. The *j,k,q,x,z* bunch do only about 1 percent of the work. Code breakers or cryptanalysts call them *rare frequency letters*.

What's this got to do with code breaking? A lot. The way letters behave gives code breakers the tips they need to break the most puzzling codes. If I knew all these tips (and I don't) it would take a book ten times this size to sort them all out. That way I'd be exhausted, and there's a fair chance you'd be bored stiff or goggle-eyed, or both.

So we'll stick to the basic ideas, and hope that you enjoy helping me unravel some minor mysteries of code breaking.

12 USEFUL TIPS

Here, then, are some "I-didn't-know-thats" to store up, before we try breaking a *substitution* code.

1. E,T,A,O,N,I,R,S, and H are high frequency letters. On the average, E shows up about 13 percent of the time, T—9 percent, A—8 percent, O—8 percent, N—7 percent, I—6.5 percent, R—6.5 percent, S—6 percent and H—6 percent.

2. The most frequent two-letter words are: AS, AT, BE, BY, DO, HE, IN, IS, IT, OF, ON, OR, SO, and TO. (Most frequent of these—OF, TO, IN.)

3. The most frequent three-letter words are: ALL, AND, ANY, ARE, BUT, CAN, FOR, NOT, THE, YOU. (Most frequent of these—THE and AND.)

4. The most frequent four-letter words are: FROM,

HAVE, THAT, THEY, THIS, WERE, WHEN, WILL, WITH. (Most frequent of all—THAT.)

5. No word in English is without at least one of these letters: A,E,I,O,U, or Y.

6. The most frequent doubled letters are: CC, EE, FF, LL, NN, OO, PP, RR, SS, TT.

7. Over half our words begin with: A,C,H,O,S,T, or W. (T the most.)

8. Over half our words end with: D,E,N,R,S,T, or Y. (E the most.)

9. The only single-letter words are I and A—and less often O.

10. U always follows Q.

11. The consonant that most often follows a vowel is N.

12. The longer a substitution code, the easier it is to break, because the high frequency letters (E,T,A,O,N,I, S,H) become more stable. But remember—letter frequencies are seldom 100 percent accurate. Sometimes, for instance, A will show up more often than T, or S more often than N.

Now, with these **12 Useful Tips** to draw from, let's tackle a typical substitution code.

GOQQON RNOMSOIYX BP QAO UKX QAKQ XJS
YKI OKPBGX RBIW QAO KIPUON QJ QABP YJWO
HOPPKDO.

First of all, how do we know it's a substitution code and not a transposition code? To find out we'll make a letter frequency count. We do this by writing out the alphabet from A to Z. Then next to each letter we write the number of times each of them appears in our coded message. In our 69-letter coded message, this is the count:

A = 4*	F = 0	K = 6*	P = 6*	U = 2
B = 4*	G = 2	L = 0	Q = 8*	V = 0
C = 0	H = 1	M = 1	R = 2	W = 2
D = 1	I = 4	N = 3	S = 2	X = 4*
E = 0	J = 3	O = 11*	T = 0	Y = 3
				Z = 0

This *is* a substitution code. If it weren't, the high frequency letters E and T would make up about 20 percent of the message. Our count shows no **E**'s and no **T**'s.

The letter that appears the most is **O**. That means that in our coded message it is probably substituted for the letter E—the highest frequency letter in the alphabet. Also, in the letter count above, I've put an asterisk next to the seven letters that appeared most often. That means there's a *chance* that code letters **O,Q,P,K,A,X,B** are substituted for the seven highest-frequency letters in our alphabet—E,T,A,O,N,I,S.

Since **O** shows up 11 times, let's substitute E for it in our code. And since **Q** shows up 8 times, let's see if it could be T—the second highest frequency letter.

```
  ETTE      E  E        T E      T   T
GØQQØN  RNØMSØIYX  BP  ØAØ  UKX  ØAKØ  XJS

    E            T E      E  T T          E
YKI ØKPBGX  RBIW  ØAØ  KIPUØN  ØJ  ØABP YJWØ

  E     E
HØPPKDØ
```

So far, so good. They seem to fit naturally into place, and we can guess at some words they might make. We now know that E equals code letter **O** and that T equals code letter **Q**.

A is the next highest frequency letter in our language, and the next two highest letters in our count are **P** and **K** —they each appear 6 times in our coded message. A little logic tells us that **P** does not stand for A. Why? Notice the code word HOPPKDO. If **P** stood for A, there'd be an AA combination in the word—and that's darn near impossible. (Aardvark is one of the few AA words I know.)

So we'll try **K**—and it seems to fit. Now this is what things look like:

```
 ETTE      E   E        T  E   A   T AT
GØQQØN RNØMSØIYX BP QAØ UKX QAKQ XJS

 A EA         T EA    E  T T          E
YKI ØKPBGX RBIW QAØ KIPUØN QJ QABP YJWØ

 E   A  E
HØPPKDØ
```

Now let's forget the frequency letters because some easier possibilities are opening up. The code word QAKQ above breaks down to T—AT. The letter H will fill that perfectly—and also fill in the two QAO code words, making them THE.

Dandy—the four H's make sense where they're inserted. So we know that code letter **A** is H.

This is the way things now shape up:

```
ETTE      E   E       THE   A   THAT
GØQQØN RNØMSØIYX BP ØⱮØ UKX ØⱮKØ XJS

A  EA          THE A    E  T TH        E
YKI ØKPBGX RBIW ØⱮØ KIPUØN QJ ØABP YJWØ

E   A  E
HØPPKDØ
```

There are still a lot of gaps to fill before we hit pay dirt, so let's look around. There's a two-letter code word BP, and a four-letter code word QABP. Item 2 on our **12 Useful Tips** list tells us that IS is a high frequency word. Put it in here and QABP spells THIS and BP spells IS. So we've knocked off two more mystery letters. Code letter **B** = I and code letter **P** = S. Now our code is starting to fall apart.

```
ETTE      E   E    IS THE   A   THAT
GØQQØN RNØMSØIYX BP ØⱮØ UKX ØⱮKØ XJS

A  EA I    I    THE A S  E  T THIS      E
YKI ØKPBGX RBIW ØⱮØ KIPUØN QJ ØABP YJWØ

ESSA  E
HØPPKDØ
```

Let's do some more looking. The code word QJ above is aching to be filled out. Since we know code letter **Q** is T—only one other letter will make sense. Code letter **J** is O. (And TO, as tip 2 in **12 Useful Tips** says, is a high frequency word.) So we'll change all the code J's to O's, like this:

ETTE   E   E   IS THE   A   THAT   O
GØQQØN RNØMSØIYX ƁƤ ØⱮØ UKX ØⱮKQ XȷS

A EA I   I   THE A S E TO THIS O E
YKI ØKPƁGX RƁIW ØⱮØ KIPUØN QȷØⱮBƤ YȷWØ

ES SA E
HØƤƤKDØ

We still have some scratching around to do. YKI is a
three-letter code word. We know **K** is A. So we look on
our three-letter frequency list (that's tip 3 of **12 Useful
Tips**) for a word with A in the middle of it. The word
CAN fits the bill, so let's try it—so that code letter **Y** is
C and code letter **I** is N. Since there are a lot of **I**'s and
Y's in our secret message, this will plug up many gaps.

Now our message looks like this:

ETTE   E   ENC IS THE   A   THAT   O
GØQQØN RNØMSØ*IYX* ƁƤ ØⱮØ UKX ØⱮKQ X*ȷ*S

CAN EA I   IN   THE ANS E TO THIS CO E
YKI ØKPƁGX R*Ɓ*IW ØⱮØ *KIP*UØN QȷØⱮBƤ Y*ȷ*WØ

ES SA E
HØƤƤKDØ

Now we can kill off a batch of other mystery letters.
The code word KIPUON is ANS_E_. If you run through
the alphabet, you'll find that only W can go after S, and
only R after E. Now we know that code letter **U** is W and
code letter **N** is R. Also, the code word UKX falls apart—
since we know it's WA_. The missing letter is Y—the only
one that makes sense in the phrase "is the way that." So
code letter **X** equals Y—and we can knock off the X's:

ETTER RE ENCY IS THE WAY THAT YO
GØQQØⱮ RⱮØMSØⱮɎX ƁⱣ QⱮØ ɄKX ØⱮKQ XⱮS

CAN EA I Y IN THE ANSWER TO TH IS
ɎKⱮ ØKPƁGX RƁⱮW QⱮØ KⱮⱣɄØⱮ QⱮ QⱮBⱣ

CO E ESSA E
ⱮⱮWØ HØⱣⱣKDØ

The rest of the message is a sitting duck. YJWO above breaks down to CO_E (R,P,M,D or V will make a word of it—but D makes the most sense.) Also, RBIW we know is _IN_—and a D fits neatly into that word at the end. In the first slot of _IND goes the letter F because B,H,K, and M make words that don't fit into the sense of the message.

So now we have:

ETTER RE ENCY IS THE WAY THAT YO
GØQQØⱮ RⱮØMSØⱮɎX ƁⱣ QⱮØ ɄKX ØⱮKQ XⱮS

CAN EA I Y FIND THE ANSWER TO TH IS
ɎKⱮ ØKPƁGX RƁⱮW QⱮØ KⱮⱣɄØⱮ QⱮ QⱮBⱣ

CODE ESSA E
ⱮⱮWØ HØⱣⱣKDØ

The code word XJS is YO_. U is the missing letter. That U also fits into the long code word RNOMSOIYX— which now breaks down into _RE_UENCY. (Tip 10 of our **12 Useful Tips** tells us that U always follows Q— so we put Q in and get _REQUENCY. And _RE-QUENCY can be nothing else but FREQUENCY.

Filling in the blanks we get:

ETTER FREQUENCY IS THE WAY THAT YOU
GØQQØN ҠNØMSØIYX ҋP QҟØ ұKX QҟKQ XjS

CAN EA I Y FIND THE ANSWER TO THIS
XKI ØKPҋGX ҠҋYW QҟØ KIPұØN Øj QҟҋP

CODE   ESSA E
YjWØ HØPPKDØ

At long last we're at the end of the trail. What's code
letter G? Try L—it makes GOQQUN break down into
the word LETTER. It also makes OKPBGX into EA_ILY
—and that can only be EASILY. To cap it all—
HOPPKDO falls apart into _ESSA_E. Only M fits the
first blank space, only G the next to last one.

Now we've got what we went after. The broken code
message is: *Letter frequency is the way that you can
easily find the answer to this code message.*

If you've survived this, you're a budding code breaker.
You've used reason and patience in equal measure, with
a bit of guesswork thrown in.

Now we'll backtrack to find out just what code you did
break. To do this find the A in the broken code message
above and see what code letter was substituted for it.
Then do B, C, D, and so on. This is what you'll come out
with:

A B C D E F G H I J K L M N O P Q R S T U V W X Y Z
K ? Y W O R D A B ? ? G H I J ? M N P Q S ? U ? X ?

Without too long a look you can see it's the Key-Word Code I showed you on page 7.

The question marks under the letters B,J,K,P,V,X and Z merely mean that those letters weren't used in this 69-letter code. If the code message had been twice as long, chances are that most of these missing letters would have been used, and the code would have been easier to break.

The very same method can be used for breaking Caesar's or Augustus's Code (though I'll show you an even quicker way to break them), Key-Word Codes, Bacon's ABC Code, The Dot Code, The Pigpen Code, The Prisoner's Code, and the Ding-a-Ling Code. Why? Because all of them—even though they use symbols or numbers or dots in place of letters—give themselves away because of the *frequency* with which individual letters appear.

In the Dot Code, for instance, if a message was long enough—say 400 letters—the longest vertical line of dots would be E, the next longest T, and so on. The *frequencies* would give it away—but it would be tougher to break than the one we just looked at.

Remember that I said Caesar's and Augustus's Codes were a cinch to break? Let me show you how.

Here's a coded message: PHHW PH DW ILYH.

Before you even take a frequency count, try this quick method of breaking it—guessing that it might be a straight substitution code like Caesar's. The method is called "running down the alphabet."

All you do is write out your message, and then continue the alphabet downward from the code words, like this:

Coded message:	PHHW	PH	DW	ILYH
	QIIX	QI	EX	JMZI
	RJJY	RJ	FY	KNAJ
	SKKZ	SK	GZ	LOBK
	TLLA	TL	HA	MPCL
	UMMB	UM	IB	NQDM
	VNNC	VN	JC	OREN
	WOOD	WO	KD	PSFO
	XPPE	XP	LE	QTGP
	YQQF	YQ	MF	RUHQ
	ZRRG	ZR	NG	SVIR
	ASSH	AS	OH	TWJS
	BTTI	BT	PI	UXKT
	CUUJ	CU	QJ	VYLU
	DVVK	DV	RK	WZMV
	EWWL	EW	SL	XANW
	FXXM	FX	TM	YBOX
	GYYN	GY	UN	ZCPY
	HZZO	HZ	VO	ADQZ
	IAAP	IA	WP	BERA
	JBBQ	JB	XQ	CFSB
	KCCR	KC	YR	DGTC
	LDDS	LD	ZS	EHUD
*	MEET	ME	AT	FIVE
	NFFU	NF	BU	GJWF
	OGGV	OG	CV	HKXG

And presto—opposite the asterisk—the message is broken. This happens to be Caesar's Code, with A substituted for D, B for E, C for F, and so on. But you can do exactly the same thing with Augustus's Code, with A substituted for B, B for C, C for D, and so forth. And this code-breaking method will work with any other straight substitution code your "enemies" might cook up. (Try it yourself with A equals Z, B equals A, C equals B, D equals C, E equals D.) Incidentally, all straight substitution codes like this are called Caesar-type codes, because he started it all by substituting A for D and so on. That's history's way of saying "thanks" to him.

Before we leave substitution code breaking and try our luck with transposition codes, there's one more thing you should know. Both the codes we've broken—plus those I said we could break by using the same method—are called *monalphabetic* codes. They're among the easiest to break because they substitute just *one* alphabet for *one* other (*mon* means *one* or *single*). In the Key-Word Code we just broke, for instance, this alphabet

K E Y W O R D A B C F G H I J L M N P Q S T U V X Z

was substituted for

A B C D E F G H I J K L M N O P Q R S T U V W X Y Z

Or, A equals K, B equals E, C equals Y, D equals W and so forth.

But cryptographers aren't satisfied to have just one alphabet to play around with, so they've devised twenty-six different alphabets to make code breakers' lives miserable. Such codes, that substitute one alphabet for *two or more* other alphabets, are called *polyalphabetic* codes. I'll show you a few of the toughest of these "poly" or "many alphabet" codes in the next chapter.

Now on to some tips for breaking transposition codes.

BREAKING TRANSPOSITION CODES

We know that the *longer* a substitution code, the easier it is to break. With transposition codes it's just the opposite—the *shorter* they are, the easier they are to break.

For instance, when you unscramble the transposed letters DTO, what word do they spell? It should take you no more than 5 seconds to come up with the word DOT.

But if I asked you what word the scrambled letters YIALCMTS can be made into, it might take you a half hour to come up with the word MYSTICAL.

The reason for this is simple. There are only six combinations of the three-letter word DOT (DOT, DTO, ODT, OTD, TOD, TDO). There are 40,320 combinations of the eight-letter word MYSTICAL.

The same holds true for words that are scrambled. *Alone me leave* is a snap to untangle—it's *Leave me alone.* But when you try this longer sentence—*Are the one the I fall the and four is of year is seasons like there most.*—the problem of putting it into its right order is far more difficult. When you scramble a whole paragraph or a full page in this way, with the commas and periods removed, breaking it becomes an almost impossible task, even though you try piecing words and phrases together into a sensible pattern.

Remember the Dirty Tricks Code on page 34? It uses this method of jumbling words to confuse a code breaker. You'll also recall that I said such a code can be broken by something called *multiple anagramming,* so now let's see how it works.

I'll give you a simple version of this code so that you'll get the idea behind breaking it. Once you have the idea, the longer and more difficult ones will be no great problem for you.

Suppose, now, that you've just intercepted this "enemy" message. You know it's the Dirty Tricks Code, but you don't have the "enemy's" key to how he has chosen to scramble and unscramble it.

AT IN CODE THE OUR SIX USUAL WILL NIGHT PLACE TOMORROW MEET CLUB.

You look it over, but no matter how you move the words around, the message stays hidden. You do note that it has thirteen words, so you store that fact away. Meanwhile, your "enemy" is giving you a horse laugh. He's stumped you.

You wait a while until you intercept this second message: THE BREAK CODE IF THIS MOST YOU ONE TO CAN INTERESTING OF IS

It, too, has thirteen words in it. Your "enemy" gives you another horse laugh. You give him a horse laugh back, then carry this second message off to your code club pals. You know that this second message, with the same number of words in it as the first message, gives you the key to breaking both of them.

Back at your clubhouse you mark the first message **A**, the second one **B**. Then you number each word of each message like this:

```
    1  2   3    4   5   6   7     8
A   AT IN CODE THE OUR SIX USUAL WILL

    9     10     11       12    13
   NIGHT PLACE TOMORROW MEET CLUB
```

1 2   3 4 5   6 7 8

B THE BREAK CODE IF THIS MOST YOU ONE

9 10   11   12 13

TO CAN INTERESTING OF IS

Now begins the detective work. You look for words in *either* message **A** or message **B** that seem to belong together and make sense.

Let's say that in message **A** you pick out OUR CLUB

WILL MEET. Over these words are numbers OUR CLUB WILL MEET. Over these words are numbers OUR
5
13 8 12
CLUB WILL MEET.

You now find the four words in message **B** with the *same* numbers over them as those in message **A**. They
5 13 8 12
turn out to be THIS IS ONE OF. Since they also make sense, you've now broken four words in each message. *This is the basis of multiple anagramming. Both messages A and B have the same number of words. Both are set in the same key order or sequence. So, when you break the code in one message, you also break the code in the other one.*

Let's take a look at messages **A** and **B** again, now that we've lifted from them OUR CLUB WILL MEET and THIS IS ONE OF.

1 2 3 4 5 6 7   8

A AT IN CODE THE ~~OUR~~ SIX USUAL ~~WILL~~

9   10   11   12   13

NIGHT PLACE TOMORROW ~~MEET~~ ~~CLUB~~

```
      1      2      3    4    5     6     7     8
B   THE BREAK CODE IF ̶T̶H̶I̶S̶ MOST YOU ̶O̶N̶E̶
```

```
   9  10         11        12 13
TO CAN INTERESTING ̶O̶F̶ ̶I̶S̶
```

This time we spot three likely words in message **B**—
```
1      6        11
```
THE MOST INTERESTING. A quick glance at message
A above shows that the same numbered words in it are
```
1  6        11
```
AT SIX TOMORROW—a phrase that makes sense. So
we've broken three more words in codes **A** and **B**. Our
messages are getting thinned out, as you can see:

```
      1 2    3      4     5   6    7        8
A   ̶A̶T̶ IN CODE THE ̶O̶U̶R̶ ̶S̶I̶X̶ USUAL ̶W̶I̶L̶L̶
```

```
     9       10        11        12       13
NIGHT PLACE ̶T̶O̶M̶O̶R̶R̶O̶W̶ ̶M̶E̶E̶T̶ ̶C̶L̶U̶B̶
```

```
     1      2      3    4    5     6     7     8
B   ̶T̶H̶E̶ BREAK CODE IF ̶T̶H̶I̶S̶ ̶M̶O̶S̶T̶ YOU ̶O̶N̶E̶
```

```
   9  10       11          12 13
TO CAN ̶I̶N̶T̶E̶R̶E̶S̶T̶I̶N̶G̶ ̶O̶F̶ ̶I̶S̶
```

Now you're so confident that you quickly try the words
```
4      7      9
```
THE USUAL NIGHT from message **A** above. The
```
                          4    7    9
```
matching words in message **B** are IF YOU TO. TO—the
```
                                        4
```
third word—doesn't seem to fit right. So we change THE
```
   7      9       4    7      10
```
USUAL NIGHT to THE USUAL PLACE in message **A**.

                                          4   7   10
Now its equivalent in message **B** is IF YOU CAN—and
that *does* make sense.

   This is how things now stand:

      1 2   3   4   5   6   7   8
 A ~~AT~~ IN CODE ~~THE~~ ~~OUR~~ ~~SIX~~ ~~USUAL~~ ~~WILL~~

      9   10   11   12   13
    NIGHT ~~PLACE~~ ~~TOMORROW~~ ~~MEET~~ ~~CLUB~~

      1   2   3   4   5   6   7   8
 B ~~THE~~ BREAK CODE ~~IF~~ ~~THIS~~ ~~MOST~~ ~~YOU~~ ~~ONE~~

      9   10   11   12 13
    TO ~~CAN~~ ~~INTERESTING~~ ~~OF~~ ~~IS~~

   As you see above, we're left with three words in each
                                   2   3   9
message. Message **A** has IN CODE NIGHT—and no
matter how we juggle these three words, they don't make
                                                    2
any sense together. Similarly, message **B** has BREAK
 3   9
CODE TO—and there's nothing accomplished by jug-
gling them. So we let them sit for a moment.

   Just to see how we stand, we take a look at the pieces
of the messages that we've already broken:

      5   13   8   12   5   13 8   12
 A OUR CLUB WILL MEET   **B** THIS IS ONE OF
      1   6   11   1   6   11
 A AT SIX TOMORROW   **B** THE MOST INTERESTING
      4   7   10   4   7   10
 A THE USUAL PLACE   **B** IF YOU CAN

Now, as we've seen, messages **A** and **B** are *almost* complete. What **A** lacks are the words that are left over, sitting and waiting to be inserted where they make sense. The same holds true for **B**. So, we insert them where they logically fit, like this:

	5	3	13	8	12			5	3	13	8	12
A	OUR	(CODE)	CLUB	WILL	MEET		B	THIS	(CODE)	IS	ONE	OF

	1	6	11	9			1	6	11	9
A	AT SIX	TOMORROW	(NIGHT)			B	THE MOST	INTERESTING	(TO)

	2	4	7	10			2	4	7	10
A	(IN)	THE	USUAL	PLACE		B	(BREAK)	IF	YOU	CAN

So here we have the two messages. **A** is *Our code club will meet at six tomorrow night in the usual place.* **B** is *This code is one of the most interesting to break, if you can.*

We've now broken this code by using multiple anagramming. In the *Quickie Code Games* chapter, you'll have a chance to try another one.

Some of the common transposition codes you're likely to run across aren't quite as tricky as the one we've just looked at. I'm thinking of the Chinese, Arab, Rail Fence, Spaghetti, Corkscrew, Farmer's Plow Path, and Rainstorm codes we saw in the *Up, Down and All Around Codes* chapter. All of these codes, and variations of them, have a *pattern* that gives them away, if you have the patience to hunt for it.

Here is a general way of breaking such codes. As I've said, it takes patience—hanging in there until you've tried every path. Even then, the code might not be solvable in this way.

Say that once again the "enemy" is trying to slip a message past you. This is it:

CUME STWP LBET ATOM

You count the number of letters in the message and find that there are 16. What two numbers multiplied by each other equal 16? The answer: $4 \times 4, 2 \times 8, 8 \times 2$. So first you try writing this message in a 4×4 pattern. You do this by putting the first four letters of the message on top, the next four under them, and so on like this:

C U M E
S T W P
L B E T
A T O M

You look over this square of letters to see if you can uncover any message. Reading up, down, across from left to right and right to left, you can see nothing that makes sense.

Next, you try setting the message 2×8—two lines of eight letters, with the first eight letters of the message on top, like this:

This time you see the message CLUB MEETS AT TWO PM when you read down from left to right, as the arrows show.

You've now broken the Rail Fence Code.

With this next intercepted message, you go through the same procedure.

MTTB PTEU OAEL WSMC

First you try the 4 × 4 approach:

You look it all over and see that the message CLUB MEETS AT TWO P.M. shows up, reading the way the arrows point, from right to left. This time you've broken the Chinese Code.

We'll try one last example of this method. The message is BULC TEEM TTAS MPOW.

Again, use the 4 × 4 approach:

Reading the way the arrows point, from top to bottom, the message CLUB MEETS AT TWO P.M. shows up again. This time you've broken the Arab Code.

Finally, you intercept one more message: CLMU ESBE AWTT OTPM. You try the 4 × 4, 2 × 8, 8 × 2 and get plenty of nothing. Your last resort is to draw a number of 4 × 4 squares and fill them in with your code message using the patterns I showed you for the Spaghetti, Corkscrew, Farmer's Plow Path, and Rainstorm codes on pages 21–22.

Here's how they'd look:

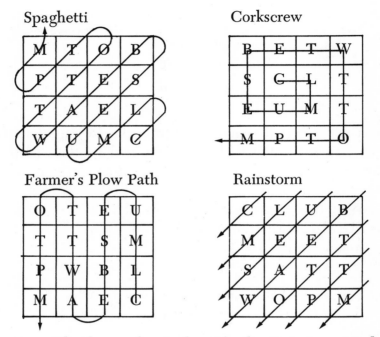

Spaghetti

Corkscrew

Farmer's Plow Path

Rainstorm

A quick glance shows that it's the Rainstorm Code you've broken.

Of course, for longer messages—say 36 letters—this whole process I've shown you takes longer. With 36 letters, for instance, there are more patterns than with 16 letters. Just so you'll know them, they're: 6×6, 2×18, 18×2, 3×12, 12×3, 4×9, 9×4.

Now you're launched as a code breaker. Or, if you prefer, call yourself a cryptanalyst. It's up to you.

And, if this taste of code breaking doesn't quite fill you, you might try Helen Fouche Gaines's book called *Cryptanalysis*. Published in 1939, it's the best book of its kind around.

Code
Tools
from Odds
and Ends

OUR COUNTRY'S National Security Agency at Fort Meade, Maryland, spends over a billion dollars a year breaking the secret communications of other nations, and safeguarding our own. This means that we Americans are part owners of such cryptographic tools as SAMOS satellites that circle the earth eyeing possible danger spots to our country's safety. SAMOS (short for **S**atellite **a**nd **M**issile **O**bservation **S**ystem) takes pictures, picks up radio and radar missile guidance signals, and relays them to our home base.

COSMOS—the Russians' eye in the sky—does the same kind of snooping, and bleeps back what's new to the Russian secret service.

Fortunately for you, the code-making and code-break-ing tools we'll be using don't come to a billion dollars. About 50 cents—give or take a dime—should get you the odds and ends you need. Yet, cheap as these tools are, all but the first I'm going to mention produce codes that are very tough nuts to crack. Of all the codes we've looked at so far, these come closest to being crack-proof.

THE SKYTALE

Back about 2,500 years ago, Spartans were the fiercest of Greek warriors. And no wonder. Spartan boys began soldiering at age 7, and kept at it for the rest of their lives. Since they never seemed to run short of enemies—Athe-nian Greeks, Thebans, Romans—the Spartans needed sly ways to shuttle secret messages among their top leaders.

To do this, their generals carried staffs of the same cir-cumference. When a general wanted to encode a mes-sage, he'd wrap leather or papyrus (paper) in a spiral around the staff and write his message on it. Let's say it was *Attack the enemy at dawn*. This is what the wrapped staff—or skytale—looked like:

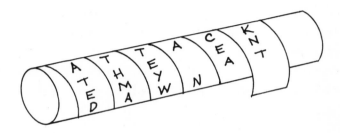

Then he'd unwrap the message and have one of his soldiers try to slip past the enemy and deliver it to a fellow general. If the soldier was captured, the enemy would end up with this baffling code in his hands:

K N T   C E A   A   N   T E Y W   T H M A   A T E D

If the message *did* get through to the other Spartan general, he simply wrapped it around his staff and the letters lined up into words that made sense.

The idea was simple, yet it fooled the enemy time after time. Even now, 2,500 years later, everyone isn't in on the secret—so try making a skytale of your own.

Here's how you do it. Get hold of a six-sided pencil. Cut out a supply of ¼-inch strips of white writing paper for your code stationery. Wrap a strip diagonally around the pencil and hold the strip in place with a rubber band. Then write your message lengthwise across the pencil.

When your friend gets it, he wraps it around his pencil and finds out what you have to say.

One caution: After the strip is taken off the pencil it stays curled, and could give the "enemy" a clue to solving your secret. So run the paper along the edge of a table or chair to take the curl out of it.

Of course, you don't have to use a pencil if you don't want to, even though pencils are easy to come by. The cardboard inside of a toilet paper roll, a dowel stick, or a cardboard cylinder you find on many metal coat hangers will do as well. Take your choice, just so you have enough of them for all of your code club friends.

If you use any of these, make your message strips about a half-inch wide. As you write your message across them, never use more than one letter on each diagonal strip or you will give away valuable hints for breaking the code (Try it yourself and see.)

If you want to put the double whammie on a would-be code breaker who you think might be wise to the skytale, encode your message with one of the key-word codes I showed you on page 6.

POLYALPHABETIC CODES

From our code-breaking chapter you know that *monalphabetic* codes substitute one alphabet for another. They're among the easiest codes to break, *if* you know how. *Polyalphabetic* codes substitute *one* alphabet for *two or more* other alphabets.

Before I show you some handy tools you can make for sending polyalphabetic codes, I want to introduce you to one more new word. It's *plaintext,* a term used over and over again by cryptographers. It simply means the message you want to send, *before* you disguise it. *Meet me in the park at seven tonight* is a *plaintext* message everyone can understand—at least everyone who can read English. When you put a moustache, dark glasses and a beard on it by setting it in, say, Caesar's Code, it comes out PHHW PH LQ WKH SDUN DW VHYHQ WRQLJKW. When it shows up in this way, as you know, we say that it's *encoded* or *set in code.*

Take a look at these twenty-six alphabets for a minute.

```
1  A B C D E F G H I J K L M N O P Q R S T U V W X Y Z
2  B C D E F G H I J K L M N O P Q R S T U V W X Y Z A
3  C D E F G H I J K L M N O P Q R S T U V W X Y Z A B
4  D E F G H I J K L M N O P Q R S T U V W X Y Z A B C
5  E F G H I J K L M N O P Q R S T U V W X Y Z A B C D
6  F G H I J K L M N O P Q R S T U V W X Y Z A B C D E
7  G H I J K L M N O P Q R S T U V W X Y Z A B C D E F
8  H I J K L M N O P Q R S T U V W X Y Z A B C D E F G
9  I J K L M N O P Q R S T U V W X Y Z A B C D E F G H
10 J K L M N O P Q R S T U V W X Y Z A B C D E F G H I
11 K L M N O P Q R S T U V W X Y Z A B C D E F G H I J
12 L M N O P Q R S T U V W X Y Z A B C D E F G H I J K
13 M N O P Q R S T U V W X Y Z A B C D E F G H I J K L
14 N O P Q R S T U V W X Y Z A B C D E F G H I J K L M
15 O P Q R S T U V W X Y Z A B C D E F G H I J K L M N
16 P Q R S T U V W X Y Z A B C D E F G H I J K L M N O
17 Q R S T U V W X Y Z A B C D E F G H I J K L M N O P
18 R S T U V W X Y Z A B C D E F G H I J K L M N O P Q
19 S T U V W X Y Z A B C D E F G H I J K L M N O P Q R
20 T U V W X Y Z A B C D E F G H I J K L M N O P Q R S
21 U V W X Y Z A B C D E F G H I J K L M N O P Q R S T
22 V W X Y Z A B C D E F G H I J K L M N O P Q R S T U
23 W X Y Z A B C D E F G H I J K L M N O P Q R S T U V
24 X Y Z A B C D E F G H I J K L M N O P Q R S T U V W
25 Y Z A B C D E F G H I J K L M N O P Q R S T U V W X
26 Z A B C D E F G H I J K L M N O P Q R S T U V W X Y
```

The top alphabet, **in bold face letters,** is the plaintext alphabet. Suppose you wanted to encode the words **HELP ME**. You could substitute them for the letters in alphabet 2 directly below it, and the encoded message would come out IFMQ NF. (That's Augustus's Code, remember?) This would be a simple, monalphabetic substitution code that the "enemy" could break by merely "running down the alphabet," as you saw on page 62. So it would be foolish to use just this one alphabet when there are twenty-six to choose from.

So, to confound the codebreakers, think of a *key number* that's easy to remember. Let's say it's 2, 4, 6, 8. Share it with your code club friends. Write this number as many times as necessary under your plaintext message, like this:

Plaintext: H E L P   M E
Key number: 2 4 6 8   2 4

We now substitute for the plaintext **H** the letter under it in the alphabet, beginning with the number 2 on our alphabet chart. This code letter is I.

E is our next plaintext letter. The number under it is 4. So we substitute for **E** the letter under it in the alphabet beginning with the number 4. The code letter is H.

L is our next plaintext letter. The number under it is 6. So we substitute for **L** the letter under it in the alphabet beginning with the number 6. This code letter is Q.

Keep going this way with the rest of the letters and you come up with IHQW NH. This coded message—or one of any length—will stop code breakers dead in their tracks. Only the most expert cryptanalyst (or maybe a mind reader) will be able to break it. Why? Because we've used *four* alphabets to encode this message. That means that *every* plaintext letter has four possible disguises instead of the *one* disguise it had in a monalphabetic code. When this happens, the letter-frequency substitution method I showed you for breaking codes falls apart—and so does the code breaker!

Remember, too, that the key number you choose determines how many alphabets, or "disguises," you'll use. The more you use, the more complex breaking it becomes, even for the best cryptanalysts around.

When your friends want to decode it, that's a different matter. They know the key number. So they do this:

Coded message: I H Q W   N H
Key number: 2 4 6 8   2 4

The letter I has the number 2 beneath it. They find the I in the 2 alphabet on the chart. The boldface plaintext letter above it is **H**.

H has the number 4 beneath it. They find H in the 4 alphabet on the chart. The boldface letter directly above it is **E**.

When your friends go on like this they come up with the original or plaintext message HELP ME.

Secure as this code is, it's a bit of a bore encoding and decoding messages, because it takes so long looking up and down long lines of letters. Besides that, all those letters make me slightly dizzy. But I showed it to you so that you'd get the idea of what polyalphabetic codes are, and how they work.

Next, though, I'm going to show you some ingenious tools for doing the same thing quickly and painlessly. Before I do, I think it would be fair to give a nod of thanks to the men who had something to do with that alphabet chart you just saw.

It was invented by a German monk, Johannes Trithemius, and showed up in a work of his called "Six Books of Polygraphy," printed way back in 1518. He called all those alphabets his *tabula recta*, Latin for "the right table or chart."

Since his way of encoding wasn't too imaginative, other men, later in the century, thought up more mysterious ways of using it. All of them were Italian—Girolamo Cardano, a doctor and mathematician; Giovan Batista Belaso, a writer; and Giovanni Battista Porta, a scientist.

But a Frenchman, Blaise de Vigenère (1523–1596), who devoted his life to cryptography, dreamed up the most baffling way to use this alphabet table. Like most scientists, he built his knowledge from studying the works of other men—especially those I mentioned—then added his own touch of genius. For this, history has given him more credit than the others. The alphabets are most often called the *Vigenere tableau* (*table* or *chart*), and his system for using it is still used. In fact, it was the one I just showed you.

THE SAINT-CYR SLIDE

The next code genius we're going to meet had more names than anyone needs. When he was born in 1835 his parents called him Jean-Guillaume-Hubert-Victor-François-Alexandre-August Kerckhoffs von Nieuwenhof. That was too much for him, so fortunately for everyone he shed most of the names and settled on August Kerckhoffs.

He made his living as a brilliant linguist, speaking Dutch, his native language, plus Flemish, English, German, French, Greek, and Latin. He also taught history and mathematics. Still, this wasn't enough to fill his active mind, so he helped to perfect a new international language called Volapük—often called "World-Speak." It was popular for a while but soon fizzed out, so he turned his mind to cryptography, and wrote one of the most famous of all books on the subject, *La Cryptographie Militaire* (French for "Military Cryptography"), in which he showed that most of the codes being used in France, and throughout the world, were easily breakable, and told how they could be tightened up.

At Saint-Cyr, the famous French military academy much like our own West Point, he promoted the use of his Saint-Cyr slide, for making and breaking codes. With this tool, he showed how just *three* alphabets, if used right, could do the work of the *twenty-six* alphabets that Vigenère used. Cryptographers thought his idea was great because it saved them time and unnecessary eye-strain.

Here's how you can make one.

Type out a plaintext alphabet, a to z, with a space between each letter. Then type out two alphabets of capital letters, from A to Z, with a space between each letter.

When you're finished with that, cut the strips out and paste the plaintext alphabet on the edge of one twelve-inch wooden ruler, the two other alphabets on the edge of another such ruler.

Now, place the working edges of both rulers so that they face each other, like this:

```
a b c d e f g h i j k l m n o p q r s t u v w x y z
A B C D E F G H I J K L M N O P Q R S T U V W X Y Z A B C D
```

The top ruler has the plaintext alphabet on it. The bottom one has the code alphabet. When you do your encoding and decoding, you slide only the bottom ruler back and forth. The top ruler, with the plaintext on it, stays put.

Now take one last look at the alphabet table on page 77 before you say farewell to it. Remember how we coded HELP ME by using the key number 2 4 6 8? Well, look at the number 2 on the alphabet chart and you'll see that the letter B is next to it. The number 4 has the letter D next to it. The number 6 has the letter F next to it. The number 8 has the letter H next to it.

So, instead of using the numbers 2 4 6 8 as our key, we could just as well have used the letters B D F H as our key. (What this all boils down to is that 1 is the A alphabet, 2 is the B alphabet, 3 is the C alphabet . . . 26 is the Z alphabet.)

With this in mind, let's set HELP ME in code by using your homemade Saint-Cyr slide. To do this we'll use the key letters B D F H in place of the key numbers 2 4 6 8.

> Plaintext: HEL P ME
> Key letters: BDFH B D

Since B is our first code key letter, we slide it under the letter *a* of the plaintext, as you see in the illustration on page 81.

Then find the *h* in the plaintext alphabet. (That's the first letter of the message *help me* that we want to set in code.) Under the *h* you'll find the code letter I.

Our next key letter is D. So slide the letter D under the *a* on our plaintext alphabet. Now find *e* in the plaintext alphabet and under it will be the code letter H.

Our next key letter is F. Slide the letter F under the *a* on our plaintext alphabet. Now find *l* in the plaintext alphabet and under it will be the code letter Q.

Our next key letter is H. Slide the letter H underneath the *a* on our plaintext alphabet. Now find *p* in the plaintext alphabet and under it will be the code letter W.

The plaintext word *help* is now encoded as IHQW. These code letters for *help* are the same as those we came up with by using the 26-alphabet chart. To encode *me*, you'd continue as I just showed you, and come up with the code letters NH.

If you understand what I've just told you, try encoding the word *good* using the key word JOHN. In other words:

Plaintext: *g o o d*

Key word: JOHN

Your answer, I hope, will be P C V Q—the coded word for *good*. Just to make sure you get this, I'll quickly review how I came up with P C V Q.

J O H N is the key word. Slide the J under the *a* in the plaintext alphabet. Find the letter *g* in the plaintext alphabet. Under it is the code letter P.

O is the second letter of the key word. Slide the O under the *a* in the plaintext alphabet. Find the letter *o* in the plaintext alphabet. Under it is the code letter C.

H is the third letter of the key word. Slide the H under the *a* in the plaintext alphabet. Find the letter *o* in the plaintext alphabet. Under it is the code letter V.

N is the fourth letter of the key word. Slide the N under the *a* in the plaintext alphabet. Find the letter *d* in the plaintext alphabet. Under it is the code letter Q.

We end up with the code word PCVQ standing for plaintext *good*.

When your friend wants to decode your message with

his Saint-Cyr slide, he simply writes out the key word
JOHN under the coded message like this:

Coded message: P C V Q
Key word: J O H N

He then slides the letter J under the *a* in the plaintext
alphabet. Next, since P is the first letter of the coded message, he finds the P on the code alphabet (the one that
slides back and forth) and above the P is the plaintext
letter *g*.

O is the second letter of the key word. He slides the O
under the plaintext *a*. Since C is the second letter of the
coded message, he finds C on the code alphabet. Above
it is the plaintext letter *o*.

H is the third letter of the key word. He slides the H
under the plaintext *a*. Since V is the third letter of the
coded message, he finds V on the code alphabet. Above
it is the plaintext letter *o*.

N is the fourth letter of the key word. He slides the N
under the plaintext *a*. Since Q is the fourth letter of the
coded message, he finds Q on the code alphabet. Above
it is the plaintext letter *d*.

That's how he uncovers the message *good*.

Once you and your friends get the hang of it, you'll
breeze along at a quick clip—encoding and decoding
messages.

I showed you earlier that you can make a Saint-Cyr
slide from two rulers. Another way that's even cheaper
is to paste the alphabets on two lengths of cardboard instead of on the rulers.

One of my young friends came up with still another

idea. His dad, an engineer, had an old slide rule sitting around the house gathering dust because he now uses one of those pocket calculators to do his problem solving. So my friend pasted the code alphabets on the moving part of it, and the plaintext alphabet above the slide. With it he zips along, making and breaking messages. If your mom or dad has an old slide rule around the house, maybe you can have it. If they're not sure, tell them you'll make them honorary members of your code club. That should do the trick.

So have fun with your new code tool. And remember, you have Jean-Guillaume-Hubert-Victor-François-Alex-andre-August Kerckhoffs von Nieuwenhof to thank for inventing it!

CODE DISKS

Code disks are as common as pancakes. In fact, if you put a little pancake on top of a big one, they'd look something like a code disk, and taste a lot better.

Because the code disks are well known to just about everyone, don't look down your nose at them. With them you can send simple monalphabetic messages or very complicated polyalphabetic ones. Disks are handy to carry with you, and are among the best of tools for writing and decoding messages with great speed. The other surprising thing about the disk is that it uses only *two* alphabets to do the work of the *twenty-six* alphabets of Vigenère, or the *three* alphabets of August Kerckhoffs's Saint-Cyr slide.

arc of circle

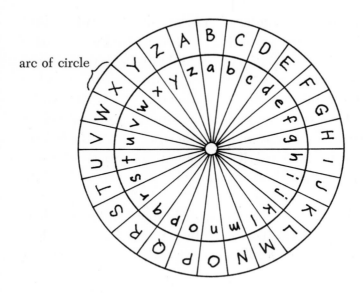

Make a code wheel by putting the metal point of a compass in the middle of the inner circle on this page. (Do
this lightly, so you don't punch a hole in the paper.) Put
the pencil point on the rim of the small circle. With this
setting, draw an identical size circle on a piece of slick
cardboard. Do this again with the larger circle and draw
it on the cardboard. Cut out both circles. Place the small
circle on top of the large one so that the center holes line
up, and push a small nail through the center holes, point
up, to hold them together. With your compass measure
an arc of the larger circle pictured above, and mark off
twenty six of them on *your* larger circle. With a ruler,
draw twenty-six lines from the center of the circles to the
arcs on the outer circle. Now, remove the nail and replace it with a paper fastener. Then write in the letters.

On your code disk, the letters on the smaller, inside circle are plaintext. Those on the outer circle are their code letter equivalents. In the drawing plaintext *a* is next to code letter B, b = C, c = D, and so on. If you do not move the inner circle, you can encode the word *cat,* for instance, with the letters DBU. (Here again, we have Augustus's Code.) But this wouldn't be making the best use of the cipher disk, even though many amateur codesters *think* this is the only way to use it.

So, now that you're wise to polyalphabetic codes, let's try encoding the plaintext word *good,* using the key word JOHN—just as we did with the Saint-Cyr slide.

> Plaintext: g o o d
> Key word: JOHN

Turn the small circle until the plaintext letter *a* is next to the large letter J in the outer circle—since J is the first letter of our key word. Now find the plaintext letter *g* (the first letter of the word we want to encode) on the small circle. Opposite it is the letter P—the first letter of our coded message.

O is the second letter of our key word. Turn the small circle until plaintext letter *a* is next to O. Now find the plaintext letter *o* on the small circle. Opposite it is the letter C—the second letter of our coded message.

Go on in this way, and plaintext *good* will end up coded as PCVQ. This is the same as we got with the Saint-Cyr slide.

Take your choice—the code disk or the slide. They're both quick and convenient, and both can produce the most baffling codes you can imagine.

When your friend wants to decode your message PCVQ, he writes the key word JOHN under it like this:

Coded message: PCVQ
Key word: JOHN

He turns the *j* (the first letter of the key word) on the small circle until it is opposite P—the first letter of the coded message. Then he finds *a* on the small circle. Opposite it on the large circle is G—the first letter of our plaintext message.

He then turns *o* (the second letter of the key word) on the small circle until it is opposite C—the second letter of the coded message. Then he finds *a* on the small circle. Opposite it on the large circle is O—the second letter of our plaintext message.

When he goes on in this way, the coded message PCVQ turns out to be *good*.

Here again, once you get the hang of it, it's quick and easy. I kept the messages short, just to show you how to encode and decode in this way. When you write long messages, just keep repeating the key word or some easy-to-remember phrase under the letters of the message you want to set in code. Do this, and unless your "enemies" have a genius among them, they will never crack your disk code.

ALBERTI'S DISK

It seems that the men who contributed the most to cryptography had talent to spare. Leon Battista Alberti (1404–1472), for example, was a gifted architect, a composer of music, a scientist, a poet, and a painter. He invented the code wheel, and was the first to use it for sending the "poly" or "many alphabet" code (although he didn't use it in the most effective way). For all this he's called the Father of Western Cryptography.

Let's take a glance at the Alberti disk, which looks something like this:

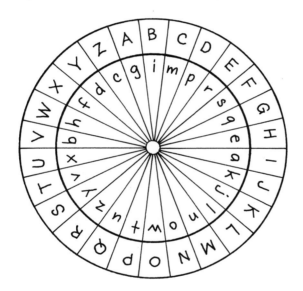

To make your own Alberti Disk, remove the small disk from the one you've already made. On its blank side write in the letters you see above, then attach it to the large circle of your disk with your paper fastener.

Notice that the plaintext alphabet on the small circle has an alphabet that *does not run in order*. When Alberti sent a coded message to a friend he would first write the letter on the inside circle that was opposite A on the outside circle. In the drawing above, that letter is *g*. So the message *Beware of the enemy* would start with g. The coded message followed, like this:

gVHOGEH NX PWH HMHCS

His friend had an identical code disk, so he just set the g opposite A on the large circle. Then he read the letters that were opposite VHOGEH, and so on, and decoded the message *Beware,* and so forth.

In those days that code was hard to break, but now we can break it by using the letter-frequency system I showed you.

Later on, Alberti thought of a better idea. He'd write four or five words the way I showed you. Then he'd turn the inner circle clockwise until *c* fell under the letter A, and write four or five words at that setting, so that the encoded message was gVHOGEH NX PWH HMHCS cJNZ TORF WIGQ YFCINZ. When he did this, he was the first man to go from a monalphabetic to a polyalphabetic code. This produced a code which was hard to break, but not nearly so hard to break as one that switches the alphabet after *every letter.* That idea came about forty years later from our friend Blaise de Vigenere.

JEFFERSON'S CODE WHEELS

Thomas Jefferson once told his children, "Determine never to be idle. No person will have occasion to complain of the want of time, who never loses any. It is wonderful how much may be done if we are always doing."

Looking back at his life, we *know* that he used his time and talents, as author of the Declaration of Independence, Secretary of State, Vice President, and later the third President of the United States, from 1801 to 1809.

Not everyone knows that he was also a superb architect and a fine violinist. And hardly anyone knows that he was the Father of American Cryptography, a title he earned by inventing the code wheels (he called the device a "wheel cipher") I'm about to describe for you.

First, let's see how Jefferson made his wheel cipher, then find out how he used it to send coded messages.

He took a wooden dowel (wood shaped like a broomstick) 6 inches long by 2 inches in diameter, and drilled a hole through the center, lengthwise. With a saw he cut the dowel into 36 pieces, each 1/6 of an inch wide— much the same way as you'd cut a piece of bologna. Now he had 36 wheels, all of them 2 inches in diameter.

He then pushed a fixed-head screw through the length, and attached a nut at the other end to hold the wheels together so that they could turn easily.

Around each of the wheels he drew a 26-letter alphabet, evenly spaced, in a random or jumbled order. (In the drawing I show only 10 wheels, each wider than what Jefferson had, to illustrate more easily his idea.)

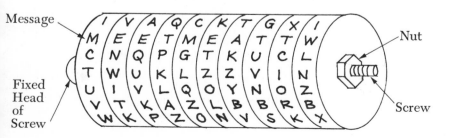

When Jefferson wanted to send the message *Meet me at two at my house,* he turned the first wheel to M, adjusted the second wheel so E was next to M, moved the third wheel so another E was next to the second E, and so forth—as you see on page 91.

He then chose any one of the remaining 25 alphabets running lengthwise across the wheel and encoded that part of his message. We'll use the bottom line of letters that shows in the illustration. So, *Meet me at tw*—the first piece of his message—came out WKPZONVSKX. He then reset his wheels as many times as necessary to complete his message, encoding them each time with any line of letters he wished.

When his friend—who had a duplicate set of wheels— received the WKPZONVSKX he set these letters in a line. Then he looked across the other 25 lines of letters for the only one that made sense and found MEET ME AT TW. It was that simple.

For each different person he communicated with in this way, Jefferson removed the 36 numbered wheels and set them in a different order that they had agreed upon. With 36 wheels, the number of ways in which the wheels can be rearranged is immense—371,993,326,789,901,-217,467,999,448,150,835,200,000,000!

No one in Jefferson's day could come close to breaking this code. It was a stroke of genius, but Jefferson never even took the trouble to patent it!

Fortunately, his idea didn't go to waste. The U.S. Army began using a wheel device, based on his idea, in 1922. By World War II they were still using a rotorized version of it.

Was his code breakable? Yes. By whom, I don't know. Whoever the man or woman or team of experts was, I'm sure it would take them a book this length to explain their system.

You can make your own Jefferson wheel cipher by following the method that I just mentioned, but it will be very difficult unless you know a cabinetmaker or carpenter who can help you. And, unless you want to send secret messages to yourself, each of your friends will have to make one, too.

I discovered that the cheapest and quickest method of making this coding tool is to get hold of eight plastic lids that fit on top of cardboard coffee cups, or what we call hot cups. When you get some lids from the dime store, stack them on top of each other the way you would a pile of quarters. You'll notice that the lids fit neatly on top of each other. You'll also see that each lid can be revolved or turned independently of the others, if you pick them up and manipulate them with your fingers. Eight lids will be plenty for your needs.

The next thing to do is type out eight different 26-letter alphabets in random order. Use capital letters and leave two spaces between each letter. An office typewriter with a wide carriage is ideal for this because you can write the whole alphabet in one line.

Now all you do is cut out these alphabet strips and glue them around the rim of your 3-inch-diameter lids. When you're finished, you'll notice that there is a gap between the first and last letters of your alphabets. Don't worry about it, it doesn't matter.

Last, number your lids 1 to 8, stack them on top of

each other, and you've got yourself a code tool for sending airtight messages. Of course, each of your code club pals will have to make duplicates of your disks.

This drawing shows you how your wheels will look when they're stacked and ready to be coded. Remember, you spell your message downward, as you see.

Camouflage
Codes

THE NAME of this chapter won't mean much to you unless you know that the word *camouflage* means to disguise someone or something. If you've ever looked for grasshoppers, you know that they're difficult to find because their green color pretty much matches the grass they're hopping around in. They're camouflaged, or hidden, by a grassy disguise.

Up to now we've talked about how to make code messages hard for an outsider or "enemy" *to understand.* Now we'll look over some ways to make such messages hard *to find.*

In case you didn't know it before, you're about to become a *steganographer.* That's a high-class word for a code maker who disguises secret messages in all sorts of ways. If that word's too heavy to carry around, just call yourself a code magician, because you'll even be able to make words disappear from sight by using invisible inks.

The lengths to which steganographers will go to slip a message by a suspicious enemy are almost unbelievable.

Herodotus, the Greek historian who lived in the fifth century B.C., tells about a man named Histiaeus who shaved his slave's head bald, wrote a message on it, and waited for the slave's hair to grow back. Then he sent his slave from the Persian court, past the sentries, to the city of Miletus with this top-of-the-head message. It went to Histiaeus's son-in-law, urging him to revolt against the Persians, and promising him help. After all that time and trouble, the plot fell through. (Why Histiaeus didn't simply *tell* the slave what to say is something of a mystery. Most likely the slave was mute or illiterate.)

Another fellow by the name of Harpagus hated the king of Medes. So Harpagus hid *his* message in the belly of a dead rabbit, disguised his messenger as a hunter, and got the message through to Cyrus, the king of Persia. In it, Harpagus promised to help Cyrus dethrone the Medean king. Together, they managed to do it.

When the ancient Chinese wanted to send a secret message, they wrote it on a very thin paper, crumpled it, and rolled it in a ball of wax. The messenger hid the wax ball in his ear, or hair, or in his mouth. If someone got suspicious of him, he swallowed the message so that he could stay alive to carry more.

Would you ever expect drawings to be used for sending secret messages from one country to another? They have been. To test how sharp your memory is, see if you can find and read the coded message in this innocent-looking drawing.

Check back to Bacon's ABC Code on page 9, and you'll see that the grass spells out a secret message. Of course, I alerted you that the picture had a message in it —but would most people think of that possibility? Probably not. (The Flip-Flop Code might have been used here, too, since it looks like a tangle of underbrush such as you see in the picture.)

If you know anything about cameras, you're aware that photos can be enlarged or reduced in size. Take a look at those picture billboards that blot out our trees and rivers along the highways and you'll get an idea of how big a photograph can be blown up. If a picture can be blown up that big, to what size can it be reduced? Early in World War II, German scientists managed to shrink photos to the size of the period you see at the end of this sentence. They called them microdots. Blown up, a microdot can easily reproduce all the words and diagrams on any page of this book!

You can imagine how Nazi secret agents, carrying little cameras, clicked pictures of secret documents, diagrams, and formulas and sent them home to Germany as microdots from countries all over the world.

When our FBI got wind of this through one of its agents, we and our allies went on a dot hunt. We found them under postage stamps, on the sticky flaps of envelopes, and as punctuation marks in letters sent by Nazi agents to and from our country. Because we were on to their trick, the threat to our national security—and that of our allies—was greatly reduced.

Secret invisible inks have been making the rounds for at least eleven hundred years. Among the Arabs, our first cryptologists, the sap from plants was a favorite. George Washington referred to secret ink as a "stain" and knew it could play a vital part in winning the Revolutionary War. The British thought so, too, because they had such inks even before we did. As late as World War II spies made secret inks from headache powders dissolved in water. Today, with huge advances made in chemistry, who can say what supersecret inks are being developed in countries all over the world!

Now that you know some of the steganographer's tricks, let's try out some for ourselves.

SAY WHAT YOU DON'T MEAN CODE

Some people are experts at saying what they don't mean. Indians say they "speak with a forked tongue." Others of us say they're "snow-job artists" or that they "talk out of both sides of their mouth." The best tag for someone who makes a habit of stretching the truth out of shape is "liar."

When I show you the Say-What-You-Don't-Mean Code, don't think I'm suggesting that you carry the idea of it over into your daily life. The code is no more than a trick, like a magician's trick, to outwit someone—just for fun.

So be on your guard. As a steganographer your job is to be suspicious of all kinds of messages.

Let's say Jim Smith has gone off to Camp Thunderbird for a week in the summer. Just so Mom and Dad won't worry about him he sends them a happy post card every day or so to cheer them up. One of his cards says:

Dear Folks,
The food at camp is super great!
Love, Jim

Jim's brother Joe looks at the card, smiles—and decodes the message from his brother. What the message really says is: *The food at camp is awful.*

Do you have any idea how Joe picked up the real meaning of this card from his brother?

Here's how.

$$|\mathcal{T}|h|e \; food \;|\,at\,|\,ca\,|\,m\,|\,p \; is \; s\,|\,uper \; g\,|\,rea\,|\,t!$$

| 1 | 1 | 5 | 2 | 2 | 1 | 4 | 5 | 3 | 1 |

I've written the message again, with vertical lines separating certain letters and pieces of words. I've also written in the *number* of letters within each pair of vertical lines.

Look back to the Prisoner's Code on page 11. In it, each letter of the alphabet has a two-digit number to identify it. The numbers above—11 52 21 45 31—spell the word AWFUL.

So far, so good. Now let's take a very careful look at the letters of the message.

Most of us *connect* the letters of a word. We'd write *The*, for instance, like this: 𝒯𝒽𝑒 . In the message above, *The* is broken into three separate letters. When the decoder sees these broken-off letters, he draws vertical lines between them, as I did.

T stands alone, so it gets a 1 under it. *h* stands alone, so it also gets a 1 under it. The letter *e* stands alone, too, but only because it's the *last* letter in the word. In the message, we can't connect it with the *f* in the word *food* because it would look phony. So, *when the last letter of a word is to be connected* with the next word, we let the end loop hang down or leave the end loop off, like this:

e = 𝑒   a = 𝑎   t = 𝓉   p = 𝑝   q = 𝑞

When we *don't want the last letter of a word to link up* with the next word, we let the end of the letter loop up as

it ordinarily does, like this: e = $\mathcal{e}$ a = $\mathcal{a}$ t = $\mathcal{t}$
p = $\mathcal{p}$ q = $\mathcal{q}$

So, in our message above, the *e* joins the four-letter word *food*, which has its letters connected, to make a total of 5. The *d* in *food* has the up loop $\mathcal{d}$ to show that *d* isn't connected to the next word.

The word *at* is connected, and the *t* has an up loop, so *at* stands for 2.

The word *camp* is broken up as *ca m p*. The *ca* is connected, and stands for 2; the *m* is separate, and stands for 1. The *p* has no loop, so it joins with *is*. Since the *s* in *is* has no loop, it joins with the *s* in *s uper* and all this stands for 4.

From there on it's easy—*uper* joins *g* and stands for 5, *rea* stands for 3, and *t* is broken from *rea* and stands for 1.

One more message, just to see that you've got the idea:

Sam's a really nice guy and we should let him in our code club now!

This breaks down into the numbers 23 15 24 43 11 43 35 54. The message: *He is a spy!* The last letter—*w*—is a null.

INVISIBLE DOT CODE

For this code, write out the very same message that you just saw and do this to it:

Sam's a really nice guy and we should let him in our code club now!

Notice that the words aren't broken into pieces as before. The dots I've inserted serve the same purpose. They break the sentence into numbers the same way the vertical lines did before—23 15 24 43 11 43 35 54. But whoever saw the dots would become suspicious that a secret message was hidden in there. If that someone knew the Prisoner's Code, he'd see that the dots break the letters into number equivalents.

So do this. Get hold of one of these invisible "inks"—vinegar, orange juice, lemon juice, grapefruit juice, Coca Cola, Pepsi Cola, 7 Up, Dr. Pepper, or just plain sugar and water. Put a few drops of whichever one of these you choose in a saucer or shallow dish. Get the smallest finishing nail you can find and dip the head (not the point) into the liquid and touch the tiny dots to the paper whenever they're needed. They'll form droplets. To help them dry, wipe off the nail head and touch it again to the droplet. (Or use a small blotter.) When the ink dries it will become invisible.

Later, when your friend gets the message, he moves it very slowly—word by word—along the top of a 100-watt (150 watts is even better) bulb and the dots will reappear as brown or black. How brown or black the dots appear will depend on how much heat he applies and which ink you choose.

The reason that these inks reappear is that they all contain carbon, which in its natural state is black. When one of these inks is heated, the compound breaks down and frees the carbon.

Lots of codesters think milk or onion juice makes an excellent ink. My experience has been that milk—low fat, high fat, or whatever—never becomes completely invisible, but leaves a glossy mark that can be seen unless you're bleary-eyed. And onion juice *does* make a good ink. But who wants to squeeze an onion? It makes you cry, and why cry if you don't have to? Besides, after you do squeeze one, you go around all day smelling like an onion.

Of course, you can *write* with all of these invisible inks I've mentioned. Don't try a worn-out ball point pen because there's always enough dried up ink on it to make telltale marks. An artist's lettering pen is no better because it scratches the paper.

I got a stick of wood about the size of a pencil, and whittled the end to about the size of a rounded pencil point. Then I dipped it into one of these inks and wrote (or I should say drew) my secret messages. For short messages these inks are swell. For long messages it's a slow process. But see for yourself.

One caution. Heat these inks on a light bulb, *not* with your mother's iron, *not* over the stove, *not* with a match or candle. If you break this rule, there's a good chance the paper will overheat, flare up, and burn you.

PRESSURE CODES

When you write anything on a piece of paper, the reason you're able to see and read the writing is that it's a different color from the paper.

Whenever you write—with a pen, pencil, or typewriter —you also *push* down on the paper and separate its fibers. This causes little depressions in the paper (much the same way as a nail point, tapped on a polished wood surface, makes little dents). Once you've made them on paper, they're there to stay—even though they are difficult, or even impossible, to see with the naked eye.

If you have a typewriter at home, put two sheets of paper in it and type a sentence or two on the top one. Then remove the sheet behind it. Hold it up in a slanting light, and you'll be able to see—and possibly read—the words on it. The reason: Pressure from the typewriter keys goes right through to this second sheet.

Now, put the paper down on a desk and rub the side of a pencil point along the almost invisible words and they'll show up clear enough to read without straining your eyes.

If you don't have a typewriter, place one piece of paper on top of another, put them both on top of a magazine (to cushion them) and write a message with a pen or pencil on the top sheet. If you push hard enough, the second sheet will get the impression. Rub it with the side of a pencil point and you'll be able to read it quite clearly. Remember, though, to print the letters—printing shows up better than cursive or script writing.

These little tricks are fun for sending secret messages past an unsuspicious person, but a keen-eyed code breaker will spot them without much trouble. So here's a gimmick to fool him or her.

Soak a piece of writing paper (not the slick, glossy kind) in your sink for about twenty seconds. Then lay it out on a flat, hard surface. Put a dry piece of paper over it and print your message on it, using a ball point pen or a pencil with a rounded tip. The writing will come through and show on the wet paper if you apply moderate pressure. Put the wet paper aside for ten minutes or so. When it dries the writing on it will disappear. To make the words reappear, wet it again.

CHEMICAL INK CODES

Up to now I've mentioned invisible inks that can be developed by heat, and pressure writing that becomes visible when it's wet. I like these methods best because the materials are easy to come by around the house and cost almost nothing.

Other inks can be made from chemicals you'll find in most chemistry sets that range from $8 on up. They're available in hobby shops, particularly the bigger ones. Most druggists won't sell these chemicals to you.

Some chemicals are colorless, or nearly so, and make excellent invisible inks. When certain other chemicals are added to them, they change to some visible color, forming what is called a precipitate.

The amounts you'll need are small. Here are two inks and developers I've tried that worked well.

The first ink is made by adding a half teaspoonful of *copper sulfate* to half a glass (4 ounces) of water. It's developed by using 1 teaspoonful of *ammonium hydroxide* mixed in half a glass of water. (Ammonium hydroxide is household ammonia.) The writing comes out dark blue.

The other ink is made by adding one half teaspoonful of *iron sulfate* to half a glass of water. Develop it by using 1 teaspoonful of *sodium carbonate* (washing soda) to half a glass of water. The ink comes out a dark brown.

I found that dipping some gauze in the developer, then dabbing it on the message—don't rub, or you'll smear the words—works well. Squeeze out the excess liquid from the gauze before you apply it to the message.

As for writing the message, it's best to use one of those small brushes that come with watercolor sets. Actually, you *paint* the words on your paper.

If you prefer to develop either of these inks with gas (*not* gas from your gas stove), try this. Pour a tablespoon of household *ammonia* into an empty milk bottle. The ammonia fumes will develop your message if you'll hold it over the top of the bottle. Just keep your nose clear of the bottle top so that you don't get a straight whiff of the ammonia fumes.

Hydrogen sulfide—made by pouring vinegar on *sodium sulfide*—will develop these inks even better than ammonia. But steer clear of this stuff. I once tried it in my mother's kitchen when I was about your age. The message came out a neat jet black—but I turned chalk white. Hydrogen sulfide smells just like rotten eggs!

Another caution: When you're finished using chemicals of any kind, store them away where your younger brother or sister cannot get hold of them. Or throw used chemicals away. Don't store them under the kitchen sink.

Last year, over 2,200 persons—one-fourth of them under five years old—died from drinking such things as drain cleaner, ammonia, bleach, fabric softener, floor wax, spray starch, and such.

Just so we don't end this chapter on an unhappy note, here's one more item for your steganographic bag of tricks.

I mentioned earlier that the ancient Chinese used to write out code messages on very thin paper and conceal them in a ball of wax. You can do the same thing by using onion skin paper that you can get from a stationery store. It's used by typists for making carbon copies of their letters.

Write your message lightly in pencil along the bottom quarter-inch edge of the paper. If there isn't room to finish the message on that side, turn the paper over and finish it on the other side. Writing small, you'll be surprised to find that you can write at least a sixty-word message in this way.

Then cut off the bottom quarter-inch strip with some scissors, and roll it around a toothpick or match stick. Instead of wax, get a small piece of putty, push down on it with your finger, lay your message in it, and roll the putty around it.

Few people would suspect that a tiny piece of putty could contain so long a message. Just toss it to one of your code club pals at school and no one will guess it's a secret message you're throwing around.

Improve Your Memory Codes

SOME OF THE greatest feats of memory I've ever heard about were performed by a man named Harry Nelson Pillsbury. From 1895 until 1900 he was our greatest American chess player, and maybe the best in the world.

He used to round up twenty-two very good chess players, seat them at chess tables set up in a circle, then walk from one player to the next making his moves. Just about every time he'd beat—or checkmate—all of his opponents. What made this an amazing feat was that he played blindfolded!

That's not all he did. Before one match, two professors thought up one of the toughest memory tests you can imagine. They wrote down this list of words and challenged him to memorize them: *Antiphlogistine; periosteum, takadiastase; plasmon; threlkeld; streptococcus; staphylococcus; micrococcus; plasmodium; Mississippi; Freiheit; Philadelphia; Cincinnati; athletics; no war; Etchenerg; American; Russian; philosophy; Piet Potgleters's Rost; Salamagundi; Oomisillecootsi; Bangmamvate; Schlecter's Neck; Manzinyama; theosophy; catechism; Madjesoomalops.*

Pillsbury glanced at the list for five seconds, handed it back to them, then recited the words in order. When they'd recovered from the shock, he shook them up again by repeating the list backward!

If you have a memory as good as his you can go on to the next chapter. Otherwise, stick with me.

Suppose I asked you to memorize the numbers 3,5,1,2, 8,9,4,6,4,7,2,9? I'm quite sure you could do it. It might take you a minute, or five minutes, or longer. It would depend on how good a memory you have, and how hard you concentrate.

On the other hand, if I asked you to memorize these numbers—1,2,3,4,5,6,7,8,9,10,11—it would be a snap. They'd stick in your mind without any effort at all.

It's easy enough to see the reason behind this. The first set of numbers is out of order. The second set is in order, the way you learned them when you were five or six years old. Another way to say this is that they're linked together or *associated*. Say 1 and what pops into your head? 2 does. Say 2, and 3 follows after.

Now, in case you don't know it, you've got the key to some of the best memory codes going—codes that you can carry around in your head.

THE 1 TO 10 MEMORY CODE

If I said *ape* or *dog* or *helicopter* or *snowflake* you could picture each one of these words in your mind's eye, because they're physical objects and sometime in your life you've probably seen each one of them. But words like *soon, idea, true,* and *easy* are impossible to visualize. We know what an *ape* looks like, but what in the world does a *soon* look like? Or an *idea?*

With what I've said in mind, we'll write down the numbers 1 through 10, and next to each number a picture word that rhymes with each of the numbers:

1 is Bun	6 is Sticks
2 is Shoe	7 is Heaven
3 is Flea	8 is Gate
4 is Door	9 is Pine
5 is Hive	10 is Hen

Now, so that these key words stick in your mind, say "1 is Bun, 2 is Shoe, 3 is Tree," and so on, five or six times. Then picture these words in your mind. Try to see a Bun, a Shoe, a Flea, a Door. When you get to Hive, think of a bee hive swarming with buzzing bees. With Sticks, think perhaps of holding them and snapping each one over your knee until each stick breaks. With Heaven, you might think of angels in the clouds. For Gate, you might think of a large iron gate that squeaks. For Pine, picture a pine tree outlined against the sky. Or think of a pine tree decorated with Christmas ornaments. For Hen, visualize a pure white hen laying a green egg.

After you've done this, write down the numbers 1 to 10. Then from memory write the key words next to them.

You'll find it's very simple. Chances are you'll remember at least 8 on the first try. If you miss any, go over them again and dream up some other links or associations.

Now, let's say you and Dad decide to do some grocery shopping. Before writing everything you need down on a piece of paper, try to *remember* what each item is.

These are the groceries you want: *a dozen eggs, a box of salt, a box of rice, a half dozen bananas, a loaf of bread, a grapefruit, shoelaces, 2 bars of Ivory soap, maple syrup, and a box of pretzels.*

A dozen eggs is your first item. *Bun,* you remember, is your first key word. Think of taking a bun in your hand and banging it down on a carton of eggs until every egg is broken. Or think of taking an egg, shell and all, and putting it between two buns and biting into this egg sandwich!

A box of salt is your next item. *Shoe* is your next key word. Think of pouring a box of salt into a shoe. Think of scooping mounds of salt off the ground with your shoe. Think of salting your shoe and eating it!

A box of rice. Key word—*Flea.* Think of eating some cooked rice and seeing a flea hop out of the rice. You say, "yuk." Think of a big flea carrying rice on his back, *fleeing* from you.

Half a dozen bananas. Key word—*Door.* Think of six doors shaped exactly like big bananas. Think of peeling the doors. Think of throwing bananas against the door until they are squashed.

Loaf of bread. Key word—*Hive.* Think of a bee hive made of a loaf of bread, with bees swarming around it.

A grapefruit. Key word—*Sticks.* Think of taking pointed sticks and driving them through a grapefruit—

and imagine the grapefruit juice squirting in your eyes.

Shoelaces. Key word—*Heaven.* Think of angels dropping shoelaces out of the sky. Think of an angel tying his shoelaces. Think of an angel tying her shoelace and breaking it.

Two bars of Ivory soap. Key word—*Gate.* Think of an iron spike gate with two bars of soap stuck on the spikes. Think of making soap from an elephant's tusk—of ivory.

Maple syrup. Key word—*Pine.* Think of a huge vat of syrup being poured over a pine tree. Think of dipping a pine tree in maple syrup and stirring it.

Box of pretzels. Key word—*Hen.* Think of a hen laying a pretzel-shaped egg. Think of pretzels all over the ground, with hens running over them and crumbling them.

You've just given your imagination a workout. All of the pictures we dreamed up were as *silly* and *unusual* as possible. They *must* be, to stay in your mind. And the more you try these mental gymnastics, the better you'll get at it. Within seconds a crowd of images, like those I've mentioned, will come into your head.

Now, to see how you did with those groceries, write down the numbers 1 to 10. Next to each one write the grocery item it stands for. I'll get you started by saying, "1 is Bun. We took the bun and squashed what?" You take it from here.

You're probably surprised at how little effort it took to call these images to mind. If you got nine or ten right, you're well on your way. If not, check those you missed, dream up a few more silly associations for them, and try again. You'll see that it works. In a way, the more images you dream up for each item, the more likely you are to remember it. It's like throwing darts at a dartboard—the more you throw, the more likely it is that one will hit the bulls-eye.

With this system you can remember up to ten items, no more. Why? Because 11,12,13 aren't rhyming words.

Yet, this system is handy and quick for everyday use. Naturally, you won't want to go through life memorizing grocery lists, so I'll tell you later how you can put key words like these to use in many other helpful ways.

If you'd *really* like to become a memory genius (or so your friends will think) you might like this next memory code even better than the first one. With it you can learn up to one hundred key words if you're keenly interested in doing so. Perhaps thirty, forty, or fifty items will be enough for you—but that's your choice.

So—to clear your mind—imagine that you've written the ten key words you've just learned on a blackboard. Now, take one of those school blackboard erasers, and mentally wipe the words off. Now your mind is cleared for the 1 to 100 Code.

THE 1 TO 100 MEMORY CODE

This code also uses numbers to tie in with key words. You'll find it's a bit more difficult to learn than the 1 to 10 Code, but once you get the hang of it, you'll be amazed at how you can remember long lists of just about anything you want to remember.

First, let's list the numbers 1 through 9 and match them up with nine different letters. Notice that all the letters are *consonants—not vowels*.

$$1 = \textbf{T} \qquad\qquad 6 = \text{G}$$

$$2 = \textbf{N} \qquad\qquad 7 = \textbf{K}$$

$$3 = \textbf{M} \qquad\qquad 8 = \text{F}$$

$$4 = \textbf{R} \qquad\qquad 9 = \text{P}$$

$$5 = \textbf{L}$$

Take a look at the number 1. It stands for the sound T. If we draw *one* heavy straight line in the T it reminds us of the number 1.

The number 2 stands for the sound N. Notice that N has *two* straight dark lines drawn in it to remind us of the number 2.

The number 3 is M. We drew the letter M with *three* dark lines so that M reminds us of the number 3.

The number 4 is R. Notice we broke the letter R into *four* dark lines to remind us of the number 4.

The number 5 is L. We drew the dark lines of the number 5 in the shape of an L, to remind us that 5 is L and L is 5.

The number 6 is G. No trouble here—number 6 looks like the letter G, and the letter G looks like the number 6.

The number 7 is K. Notice that the K is drawn half dark and half light. The dark half of the K looks like the number 7 that has fallen down. Turn the book a quarter turn clockwise and the dark 7 in the K will be standing upright.

The number 8 is F. We stuck the F inside the top loop of the number 8 because it forms an odd enough looking symbol to remind you that 8 is F and F is 8.

The number 9 is P. No trouble here—9 looks like a backward P, and P looks like a backward 9.

Now, look over these letters and numbers until you know all nine of them. The drawings of the letters will make it fairly easy to link them up with the right numbers. When they sink into your head, you've taken a giant step toward learning this most useful code.

Okay, then, let's say you now know the letter-number link-ups. The next step is to learn the nine key *words* I'm going to give you. Notice that the key words *start* with the *key letters* we just learned for each number:

1 = **Tea**	6 = **Guide**
2 = **Navy**	7 = **Key**
3 = **Ma**	8 = **Fuzz**
4 = **Red**	9 = **Pa**
5 = **Lid**	

Now let's try to stick these key words in our mind, like pins in a pin cushion.

1 = T = Tea. Easy. The letter T sounds like the word Tea.

2 = N = Navy. Think of *two* Navies with their *two* ships painted with the number 2 on them.

3 = M = Ma. *Three* Ma's greet you when you come home from school. All three look exactly like your Ma. So you yell "Ma, Ma, Ma."

4 = R = Red. *Four red* rhymes with forehead. Think of *four* red heads of hair.

5 = L = Lid. Think of *five* Lids of different sizes running around looking for the right size pots to fit onto.

6 = G = Guide. Think of *six* guides gazing in six directions—up, down, north, east, south, and west.

7 = K = Key. Think of the number 7 with *seven* keys on it, jangling along while it hops on one leg.

8 = F = Fuzz. Think of stuffing the number 8 into a huge pile of fuzz. Think of 8 with fuzzy whiskers.

9 = P = Pa. Imagine your Pa shaped like the figure 9. You say to him, "Pa, watch your posture."

Go over these linkups until you're sure you know all nine of them. If one or two don't seem easy to remember, dream up some associations of your own—the more the better. When you can say all nine letters and numbers and key words in two minutes, you're doing fine. Later on, with practice, you'll be able to say them in a minute or less.

We know the first nine key words. Or let's say we do, so we can go on. But how do we form our tenth word, and our eleventh, and twelfth, right through to one hundred? Easy.

The number ten is written 10, right? Think back to what letter the number *1* stood for. It was *T*. How about the number 0? We never did give you a letter to match it, but we will now. From now on, the *number 0* will always equal the *letter S*. The best way to remember this is to remember the Morse Code distress signal, SOS . . . SOS . . . SOS . . . . That way you'll easily remember that all number 0's equal the letter S.

Now we've put it all together. We substitute the letters TS for the number 10. But TS isn't a word, so we drop in a couple of vowels—and TS becomes ToeS. Get the idea?

How about the number 11? What key word can you

make out of it? Again, remember that the number 1 is the equivalent of the letter T. So the number 11 becomes TT. Stick in a vowel and TT becomes ToT—our eleventh key word, meaning a small child.

Now let's see what we can do with the number 12. The number 1 is T. The number 2 is N. Put them together and you have TN. Stick in a vowel and you have word number 12—TiN. (Of course we could have made the word ToN, but it wouldn't have been a picture word. TiN you can see, ToN you can't see.)

How about the 13th key word? Again, the number 1 is T. The number 3 is the letter M. Put them together and you have TM. Here again, we could make TM into ToM or TiMe—but neither is a picture word. So we'll try TiMer, a stopwatch used for timing sporting events.

One more example should clear up any question about this system. Number 14 is equal to the letters TR. TRain should do it.

Now let's see what our first twenty key words and numbers turn out to be.

1 = **Tea**	11 = **ToT**
2 = **Navy**	12 = **TiN**
3 = **Ma**	13 = **TiMer**
4 = **Red**	14 = **TRain**
5 = **Lid**	15 = **TaiL**
6 = **Guide**	16 = **TiGer**
7 = **Key**	17 = **TicK** (The bug that bites you)
8 = **Fuzz**	18 = **TaFfy**
9 = **Pa**	19 = **ToP** (The kind you spin)
10 = **ToeS**	20 = **NoSe**

Look over the twenty-word key list for about two minutes, and then try this. Say, "What is 19?" The letters TP
must come to mind if you remember the link-ups. What
word do you make of it? Look at our list to see if you're
right. Try 20. Two is N and the number 0 is always S.
NS becomes what word? Look at our list to see if you've
come up with the right answer.

By doing this you'll see that most of the time you will
come up with the word on the list. Why is this? Well,
most of our words are short. Most have vowels as the
second letters in the words. All are picture words. And
last, given the two letters NS, there aren't too many
words that easily come to mind—so your chances of hit-
ting the right one are pretty good.

Now, just for the fun of it, take a stab at the number
85. We haven't yet listed a word for it, but see if you hit
on the one I'll list a bit further on. The number 8 is F.
The number 5 is L. FL suggests what word? It's short.
Its second letter is a vowel. Write out your word, then
check the list that follows to see if you've hit the right
key word. Notice I said the "right" word, because the
words I'm listing work best for me. But you needn't use
all of *my* words. There's a good chance that you'll come
up with picture words of your own, that you find easier
to remember.

Or try the number 56. Five stands for the letter L. Six
stands for the letter G. LG is the combination. What
word comes to mind? If you said LeG, you're right. (Lag
or Lug wouldn't be as good, because they aren't words
you can picture easily. But LeG is common, and something we see every day.)

I did this to show you how the number combinations
readily call certain words to mind.

I'll give you the remaining eighty words. Look at each word just once and try to picture it. Don't pay much attention to the number in front of it. When you look at MuG, for instance, think of a drinking mug or cup made of brass, or of glass. Think of crashing it down on a table and shattering it. With MiRror, think of looking in a mirror and seeing yourself. Think of smashing the mirror. For FeMale, picture some one special girl or woman that you know. Think of her laughing, crying, running, walking. With LaKe, think of jumping into a calm lake and causing a big splash. Think of moonlight on the lake. This is merely a way of bringing these words to life so that you remember that you've seen them.

Here they are. I'll explain any that I think need explaining.

21 = NeT

22 = NuN

23 = NaMetag

24 = NuRse

25 = NaiL

26 = NiaGara (Falls)

27 = NicKel (The coin)

28 = NiFe (It's really kNife, but it sounds like NiFe. I used it because no other picture word could be found for the NF combination.)

29 = NaPkin

30 = MiSt

31 = MiTt

32 = MiNe (A coal or gold mine)

33 = MuMmy

34 = MiRror

35 = MaLlet (A wooden headed hammer)

36 = MuG

37 = MiKe (A microphone)

38 = MaFia (Think of a mob of gangsters with guns)

39 = **MaP**
40 = **RaSp** (A large rough type of file)
41 = **RaT**
42 = **RiNk**
43 = **RooM**
44 = **R.R.** (A railroad)
45 = **RoLl** (A bun or pastry)
46 = **RaG**
47 = **RocK**
48 = **RaFt**
49 = **RiP** (A tear in a sheet)
50 = **LeTtuce**
51 = **LoT** (A piece of ground)
52 = **LiNe** (String or clothes line)
53 = **LiMb**
54 = **LuRe** (A fishing lure)
55 = **LiLy**
56 = **LeG**
57 = **LaKe**
58 = **LiFt** (British for elevator)
59 = **LiP**
60 = **GaSpipe**
61 = **GuT** (Intestine)
62 = **GuN**
63 = **GuM**
64 = **GaRter**
65 = **GoaL** (A football goal post)

66 = **GoGgles** (Eyeglasses)
67 = **GooK** (A gooey mess of some kind)
68 = **GaFf** (A spear for hooking a fish)
69 = **GuPpy** (A minnow, or small fish)
70 = **KiSser** (Slang for a face)
71 = **KiTe**
72 = **KiN** (Think of a special relative of yours)
73 = **KiMono** (A loose robe or gown)
74 = **KeRnel** (A grain of corn)
75 = **KiLn** (Stove or oven)
76 = **KeG**
77 = **KicKer**
78 = **KoFfee** (It's really coffee, but koffee sounds the same. KF is hard to make into a picture word)
79 = **KiPper** (A fish)
80 = **FiSt**
81 = **FooT**

82 = FaN (A machine for cooling the house)

83 = FeMale

84 = FiRe

85 = FiLe (A fingernail file)

86 = FiG

87 = FaKir (Think of a turbaned Indian standing before a cobra)

88 = FiFe (A flute)

89 = FoP (Think of a dandy dresser)

90 = PoSt

91 = PiT (A peach or plum pit)

92 = PeN (A writing pen)

93 = PiMple

94 = PeaR

95 = PaiL

96 = PiG

97 = PicKle

98 = PuFf Adder (A poisonous snake)

99 = PoPcorn

100 = TiSSue

Right now get a piece of paper and write down these numbers: 2,16,27,33,44,57,63,78,84,93. If you remember more than half of the words these numbers represent, you're doing very well. With time and a little practice, you'll soon know all one hundred numbers.

What use can you make of these key words? You could learn the names of all 38 presidents of the United States from Washington to Gerald Ford. You could learn the key phrases of the Bill of Rights and all the other amendments to the Constitution of the United States. You could learn the names of the original 13 states of the union, or the names of all 50 of our states in alphabetical order— or in any order you wanted. You could learn geography —the countries in South America, in Africa, or the provinces of Canada. There's just no limit.

If you're going to make a speech in class, three or four key words can remind you of key thoughts in the speech and save your writing it out.

Later on, in our *Quickie Code Games* chapter. I'll show you a fun game to play using these codes.

If you're wondering how you'd remember the names of the Presidents of the United States, using our key words, here's an example of how it's done.

Your first key word is *Tea*. The President—*Washington*. Imagine *washing* yourself with tea. *Washing* sounds like *Washington* and calls the name to mind.

Second key word is *Navy*. *Adams* was our second President. Picture a navy of ships falling over *a dam*—picture *a dam*. *Adams* sounds like *a dam*.

Third key word is *Ma*. Picture a tiny *son* carrying his mother. Tattooed on his chest is *Jeff*. *Jeff-son* sounds like *Jefferson*, our third President. Get it?

Even though Washington, Jefferson, and Adams aren't the best of picture words, you can remember them if you're inventive enough. Certain other presidents' names would be easy as pie to remember—Ford, Lincoln, Buchanan (sounds like cannon), Hoover (vacuum cleaner). See why?

But let's suppose you wanted to remember the original 13 states of the union. It could work this way:

Tea is the first key word, *Massachusetts* the first of the original 13 states. Think of Tea being served at *Mass*. Imagine a priest sneezing *Choo*. *Mass-Choo* sounds like Massachusetts.

Navy is the second key word. *Rhode Island* is the next state. Picture a navy—ship after ship—on a dry *road*. Picture an *island* with only one huge *road* on it, with ships from the navy on that road.

You can take it from here—if you'll put your imagination to work.

REMEMBER-THE-NAME CODE

Suppose ten people you'd never met before walked up to you one by one and introduced themselves to you. How many of their names do you think you could remember?

If you said three, you'd be doing about what the average person can do. But being average isn't good enough for you, so if you'll pay attention for the next few minutes, you'll be able to improve your ability to remember by about 100 percent.

To prove my point, cut out pictures of ten different people from a magazine, tape them to a piece of paper, and let Mom and Dad make up phony last names for each of them and write these names under each picture.

When they've done this, have them show you the names *and* faces for *two minutes*. Then they're to show you the picture of each person, one by one, covering the name under each one to see how many you can remember.

Most people who try this test get shaken up. The thought of remembering ten people in two minutes *seems* so difficult that their minds go blank. Others stay cool and do fairly well. I don't know how you'll make out, but jot down your score. And don't worry if it isn't so hot— even if you don't remember a single name.

Now, let's see how you can improve your score the next time you take this kind of test.

One reason most of us are poor at remembering names is that we *lack confidence* in our ability. If we start out with this feeling we're bound to fail—at remembering names or at anything else.

Another reason we may forget a person's name when we're introduced is that we may never *really* hear the name. It goes in one ear and right out the other, nonstop. Perhaps we ignore the name *and* the person who has it. (It's a way of being ignorant and rude, all in one.) And we look at the person without really seeing him or her. For instance, was he tall or short, thin or fat, did he limp or stutter, smile or frown? Did he wear glasses? If so, what color and shape were they? What color were his eyes behind those glasses? Did his ears stick out or were they close to his head? What shape was his nose? Did he have thin or thick lips? And so on. Usually, when we look at people, we don't consciously pay attention to these things I've mentioned.

And last, the chances are that you never tried the best remembering method of all—associating the name with the way a person *looks* or *acts*. I call it the Remember-the-Name Code.

So, to become a memory expert for names, you *must:*

1. Be *absolutely confident* that you can remember *any* name *quickly*.

2. Pay attention to each person you meet. (I don't mean that you should stand and stare at people until they feel uncomfortable, but do talk and be friendly while you do your people-watching.)

3. *Link up* or *associate* the name with the way he or she *looks* or *acts*.

OK then, let's try some of these ideas to see how they can help you out.

Suppose you meet a Mr. Silverman. You look him over and note—among other things—that he walks very

straight. That his hair is gray—or *silver*. Imagine yourself pouring a vat of liquid silver over his head so that
it runs down all over him, hardens, and stops him in his
tracks. You've just made him a *silver man*. Picture him
that way.

Or how about a Mrs. Saltinstall? You notice that she
smiles a lot and has beautiful white teeth. Imagine her
gargling with *salt* water. Imagine her getting too big a
mouthful of salt, sputtering, and running off to her car.
She jumps in it and it *stalls*. These two sounds—*salt-stall*
—or just one of them, will recall her name to you the
next time you see her.

How about a Mr. Franklin? Try this name yourself
first, then see if some of your associations are the same
as mine, even though they don't have to be the same.

This is what came to my mind. I imagined Mr. Franklin flying a kite—the way Ben Franklin did. Mr. Franklin
mentioned that he likes to eat—so I imagined him eating
a 3-foot-long *Frank* with *lint* all over it. (Don't worry
about calling him Mr. Hot Dog the next time you meet
him.) Since Mr. Franklin says what's on his mind—I
knew that he was *frank*—or outspoken.

We'll try one more—a Mrs. Mussel. *Mussel* sounds like
muscle. Mrs. Mussel is skinny, about ninety pounds.
That's what stays in your mind after you've looked her
over. You imagine her flexing her right arm *muscle* and
you're amazed that the *muscle* is huge—bigger than all
the rest of her. (Another thing to remember is to get *action* into your mental pictures. Things in motion are
easier to see than things that stand still.)

Now, just for practice, look at the names and faces of

some people in the newspaper. Practice these link-ups to make you remember their names.

Some names you'll find are simple to remember—like Lincoln, Graves, Pepper, Hammer, Brown, Greene, West. Others *seem* hard—Skibitski, Pappalardo, Lippincott, Stefanelli—until you break their names into action syllable pictures. If you do this, you'll find that longer names often stick better than the short ones.

With this new knowledge in your head, ask Mom and Dad to try a new ten-name test the same as the first one, but with different faces and different names.

When you're finished, compare this score with the score you got on the first test. I'm quite sure test two will come off far better than the first, if you give it a real effort.

With a few weeks' practice you'll find that you're excellent at remembering names. That will give your self-confidence a big boost, and serve as a compliment to all those people whose names you remember.

Quickie
Code
Games

WITH MOST games we play we compete against one or more of our friends. That's fun, and it's the usual way of doing it.

But it's also valuable for us to compete against ourselves by testing our skill at something we've learned—or think we've learned. It's also a way of keeping us on our mental toes; of always doing our best at whatever we try.

Most of the code games I'm about to show you can be played in either way. That's up to you. They're taken from different parts of the book, and I've noted on which pages they appear, just in case you have to refresh your memory.

The answers are on page 131 of this chapter, for those games that require an answer.

So good luck. Enjoy a few laughs—whether you try these games by yourself or with some friends.

Reference: Pages 61–63. Each of these are Caesar-type codes that can be solved by "running down the alphabet." See if you can get the joke.

1. Confucius says: Man who bowl perfect game needs
   BC HWAS HC GDOFS
2. What do you do when your boat sinks? VGPQ
   HDBT HDPE PCS LPHW NDJGHTAU PHWDGT
3. Old fishermen never die—CQNH SDBC BVNUU
   CQJC FJH
4. Confucius says: Man with forked tongue should
   YPGPC VTDD MLWWZZY

Reference: Pages 42–46. Try to solve these Pigpen and Tic-Tac-Toe Codes.

5. Daffy definition: A cannibal is a person
   ⵎⵏⴲ ⵌⵎ ⴲⵕⵄ ⟨⅂ ⴸⵌ⟩ⵌ ⅂ⵕⴲ ⅂ ⵡⵕ
6. Why is it wrong to whisper? Because
   ⵌ⟩ ⵌⴸⵕⵕⵄ ⅃ⵡⵡⵄ ⴸⵕⵄ
7. How did they finally catch Dracula? He was
   ⴲⵀⵄⵌⵄⵌⴸⵕⵒⴸⴲ ⅃⟩ ⟩ⵎⵔ ⵡⵡⴲⴲⵄ ⵡⵡⵔⵡⵡⵡ
8. Show me a short sculptor and I'll show you a
   ⵔⵔⵄⵌ⋅ⵌⵔⵏⵒⵄ ⵌⵌⵡⵡⵡⵌⴲⵎⵒⵡⴲ
9. Daffy definition: A store detective is
   ⵌ ⵌⵔⵒⵔⵒⵌⵔⵎⴲⵌⴲⵌⵌ

Reference: Pages 39–40; 46–48. Solve these Flip-Flop and Ding-a-Ling Codes.

10. Why couldn't Batman go fishing?
    SⵛR·MⴍH⅂⅂ⵌⴰⵎⵌ⟨N—ᗺ·R

11. Daffy definition: Surfer—a MⱯNOVⱶꓤ◖ΘꓛꓷⱯꓤꓷ
12. How would you send a message to a Viking? 873 66773 2633
13. Old bankers never die, they 5878 5673 46837378

Reference: Pages 48–51. Do you remember your Jargon Codes?

14. Who invented the first plane that didn't fly? E'THAY ONG'WRAY OTHERS'BRAY
15. Drip: Can you stand on your head? Drop: No. ABITS TABO'ABO HABIGH
16. When do you put a frog in your sister's bed? WOP' HOP'ENOP YOP'OU COP'A'NOP'TOP COP' ATOP'COP'HOP A MOP'OU'SOP'E
17. What did one shrub say to the other? BUBO'YUB A'MUM I BUB'U'SUS' HUTCH'E'DUD

Reference: Pages 52–61. This is a monalphabetic substitution code. Can you break it?

18. JLUVNZUVJ NYVDV PDV KLRV ADLQOVUJ NYPN FV WZTR EVDH RZWWZKMON NL JLOEV ZT NYV QVXZTTZTX, QMN FZNY YPDR FLDC PTR APNZVTKV FV JLLT JVV NYV PTJFVD.

Reference: Pages 64–69. Solve the two coded jokes below, using multiple anagramming.

1	2	3	4	5	6	7
19. GET | GET | IN | SAY | DRINK | IN | CONFUCIUS

8	9	10	11	12	13
PUNCH | MAN | FACE | NOSE | FRUIT | WHO.

1	2	3	4	5	6
20. SLEEP | UP | RAILROAD | SAY | WAKE | SPLIT

<pre>
    7   8   9   10   11
CONFUCIUS WITH MAN ON PERSONALITY
   12   13
TRACKS WHO.
</pre>

Reference: Pages 11–17.

21. You receive this message in the Nihilist Number Code—74 49 86 66 97 78 76 53 96 68 94 65 85 68 94. Your keyword is WORM. Decode the message.

22. See if you can get the punch line for this joke that's coded in the Prisoner's Code: Doctor: Don't you know that my hours are from two P.M. to four P.M.? Patient: Yes but 4423151434224423114412244432151424143344. (See if you can do this one from memory.)

Reference: Pages 23–24.

23. This is a well-known transposition code message: TEECRI CDIAOD SHHLST HFNEAL OESSLA TEILPL. Break the message and tell what transposition code it is.

Reference: Pages 76–88.

24. There's a joke hidden in this polyalphabetic code that can be solved by using the Vigenère Tableau, the Saint-Cyr Slide, or the Code Disk. Your key phrase is "NEW YORK CITY." The message FMCL WE K YIMAU VANOZB UPHN—VJ ER RFOUVM RVGG RCTU VW NQ.

Reference: Pages 113–115.

In the 1 to 100 Memory Code, see if you can remember:

25. The first nine key letters

26. The first nine key words

27. Using the 1 to 100 Memory Code, try to memorize

the suits—spades, hearts, clubs, diamonds—of thirty cards from a deck of playing cards. (Do this by placing the deck face down, turning over one card at a time. Then place the thirty face-up cards back, face down, on the deck, after you've looked at them. Last, name the suit, and check your answer by turning the cards face up again.)

Answers:

1. Confucius says: Man who bowl perfect game needs *no time to spare.*
2. What do you do when your boat sinks? *Grab some soap and wash yourself ashore.*
3. Old fishermen never die—*they just smell that way.*
4. Confucius says: Man with forked tongue should *never kiss balloon.*
5. Daffy definition: A cannibal is a person *who is fed up with people.*
6. Why is it wrong to whisper? Because *it isn't allowed.*
7. How did they finally catch Dracula? He was *overdrawn at the blood bank.*
8. Show me a short sculptor and I'll show you a *low-down chiseler.*
9. Daffy definition: A store detective is *a counterspy.*
10. Why couldn't Batman go fishing? *Robin ate all the worms.*
11. Daffy definition: Surfer—*a man overboard.*
12. How would you send a message to a Viking? *Use Norse code.*
13. Old bankers never die, they *just lose interest.*
14. Who invented the first plane that didn't fly? *The Wrong brothers.*

15. Drip: Can you stand on your head? Drop: No *it's too high*.
16. When do you put a frog in your sister's bed. *When you can't catch a mouse*.
17. What did one shrub say to the other? *Boy am I bushed*.
18. SOMETIMES THERE ARE CODE PROBLEMS THAT WE FIND VERY DIFFICULT TO SOLVE IN THE BEGINNING, BUT WITH HARD WORK AND PATIENCE WE SOON SEE THE ANSWER.
19. CONFUCIUS SAY: MAN WHO GET FACE IN FRUIT DRINK GET PUNCH IN NOSE.
20. CONFUCIUS SAY: MAN WHO SLEEP ON RAILROAD TRACKS WAKE UP WITH SPLIT PERSONALITY.
21. Get out of town now.
22. Doctor: Don't you know that my hours are from two P.M. to four P.M.? Patient: Yes but *the dog that bit me didn't*.
23. The Fence Rail Code is as old as the hills (ptl—nulls).
24. SIGN IN A WATCH REPAIR SHOP: IF IT DOESN'T TICK, TOCK TO US.
25. First nine key letters are: T,N,M,R,L,G,K,F,P.
26. First nine key words are: Tea, Navy, Ma, Red, Lid, Guide, Key, Fuzz, Pa.

Index

133